Ruth and Naomi

RUTH AND NAOMI

A Story of Friendship, Growth and Change

Elizabeth Ruth Obbard, O.D.C.

ST. ANTHONY MESSENGER PRESS

Cincinnati, Ohio

Scripture citations are taken from *The New Revised Standard Version Bible*, copyright ©1989 by the Division of Christian Education of the National Council of Churches of Christ in the U.S.A. and used by permission.

Cover art: A variation on *The River* by Lee Lawson, copyright ©1987
Interior photo art by Gene Plaisted, o.s.c.,
    copyright ©The Croisers/Gene Plaisted, o.s.c.
Cover and book design by Mary Alfieri

ISBN 0-86716-503-0

Published by St. Anthony Messenger Press
www.AmericanCatholic.org

Printed in the U.S.A.

FOR ALL THOSE
who have been
with me on my own
Ruth journey,
With gratitude for
so much loving
kindness and truth

Contents

Foreword

M r. and Mrs. Briggs lived at "44 Silcoates Lane, Kirkhamgate—near Wakefield—Yorkshire." My brother Robbie and I chanted the address we knew by heart to anyone who would listen as we traveled north each year for our summer holiday. We were a shy, close-knit twosome, taken up to Victoria Station from Hindhead in Surrey by Nanny, escorted in a taxi across London to St. Pancras and there placed in the train under care of the guard for the last lap of our journey.

At Wakefield Station, the couple we had been instructed to call "Granny and Grandpa Briggs" would be waiting in their best clothes, "Grandpa" with tears streaming down his face and his hands shaking from Parkinson's disease. "Granny," the stronger of the duo, would be in her usual buttoned-up-to-the-neck coat sporting a brooch of marcasite, her eyes misted over and dabbed at occasionally with a handkerchief that displayed a crocheted border poking its white triangle out of the breast pocket of her suit. It was the predictable beginning of summertime in a strange land, and it ended only with the close of the holidays. All was unfamiliar to two children from the south of England—the Yorkshire accents, the village gossip, the people we met and to whom Granny would show us off in our private school blazers. They would duly enthuse about our growth and our "posh voices" which at home were accepted as totally normal.

How could this strange couple be friends of the family? Where could they have met our father and what on earth had they in common? They lived in a working-class world that struck me as storybook-like the minute we came in the back door of 44 Silcoates Lane. We then stepped straight into a tiny kitchen which led into a living room smelling permanently of long buns and canned salmon. Everyone sat in this room where a coal fire was lit all year round. Everyone ate in this room, entertained in this room, listened to the always-on radio in this room, not like our own home where we had rooms for everything, each with its own furniture and purpose, and where children were strictly segregated from the adults. The unused front room of Granny's house held an upright piano, and we would go in there sometimes while Granny played and sang amid the vases of plastic flowers and plush chairs that no one sat upon.

Upstairs there were three bedrooms. One for Granny and Grandpa with a big double bed; one for me, a very feminine room with another double bed, and with cut glass containers on the dressing table. On the wall was a black silhouette on silver paper depicting Narcissus looking at himself in a forest pool. This must have been a young woman's room at some point in its history and I was fascinated by who she might have been and what she might have been like. Then there was a tiny box-like room for my brother and a bathroom. This house didn't have hot water on tap like ours, but a something called a geyser that heated our water on bath nights. It was so hot we had to be carefully supervised as we got in and out of the tub.

On the piano in the front room was a photograph of "Granny's dead daughter" with Robbie in her arms. The picture showed her half-length in a sitting position: a beautiful woman with upswept hair, her cheek against my brother's cheek, both with secretive half-smiles. He was wearing a fine hand-smocked romper suit and must have been just a few months old. There were only thirteen months separating Robbie and me, but there were no pictures of this beautiful woman with another baby. It seemed unbelievable that such a storybook creature could be related to dowdy old Granny and Grandpa— her beauty, her sophisticated gown, her evident self-possession didn't fit in somehow. It was all part of the great mystery of 44 Silcoates.

Granny was a big, sensible woman, who had left school at fourteen to work in the mills of Darwen. Grandpa was small and weak, partially deaf as a result of sleeping out in the fields with horses during the First World War when he was a member of the veterinary corps. His prized possession was a Joan of Arc tiepin which he had acquired at Rouen. He never spoke of those days, and I suspect the combination of large animals (he was no lover of pets or wildlife in any form) and cold air had damaged more than just his hearing. He, too, had left school at fourteen and worked in the mills. He was the youngest child of eight, his father a miner, but such a career was unsuited to his delicate health. When he and Granny married they began to work for the Post Office, and had eventually acquired their own business outside Leeds. He presently worked as a handyman at Wakefield Art College. Some-times we would walk over the fields into Wakefield with him and see his den and the little store where he sold drawing books he had cobbled together from stray pieces of white paper. How were we children part of this world? Why were we here? What on earth made our parents send us all this way each summer?

In time the truth dawned: Granny and Grandpa were our real grandparents after all. Their daughter was our real mother, not the woman we called Mummy who lived at home with Daddy and who seemed so distant when compared with the mothers of our friends. We spoke of our discovery in hushed whispers walking along the seafront at Morecombe, where Granny's brother had a bungalow for weekends when he wasn't selling pies in his Darwen cafe.

Much later, I learned more of our mother, each piece of the picture jealously hoarded and worked over in my imagination. She was an only child named Ida, the prized daughter of working-class parents who wanted their girl to have all they could give her and more. She grew up with beauty and style, and through her work gradually came to mix with people of another social stratum. At length she fell in love with and married a rich Scotsman, whereupon she went up to the Highlands to live in a grand house. But the marriage was unhappy. Her husband proved to be an alcoholic (dreadful for Ida's parents, who were strict Methodists and never touched so much as a sip of wine). What was even worse, Ida divorced him in an era when divorce was anathema. She was still in her early twenties and could not face a lifetime attached to a man who drank, however rich and influential he might be.

To get away from her past, Ida joined the Admiralty as a private secretary and sailed for India and East Africa to see the world. It was in India that she met my father, a recently bereaved Army officer in his thirties, whose wife Jessie had died in childbirth. My father came from a long line of career army officers and had himself been born in Burma and educated in England. He had had no home life to speak of. His situation was ripe for another marriage and theirs took place in Bombay. Two lonely people had found one another and formed a new union.

Pregnancy followed swiftly, and Ida returned to England with her husband for the birth of my brother Robbie in Wakefield. Then another pregnancy, this time in Kent while my father was abroad in Germany. All seemed ready for a successful delivery when things began to go badly wrong. The child was breech, a lot of blood was lost, peritonitis and puerperal fever set in and my father was called back to a dying woman of twenty-nine, when he had lost another young wife scarcely five years earlier.

Since Ida was their only child, my grandparents never got over their loss. Grandpa traced his Parkinson's to the time of her death. What is worse, Granny told me that Grandpa felt God had punished Ida for her divorce.

My brother and I were sent to Jersey to be brought up in our paternal grandmother's home, attended by a nanny. When my father married again we were three and four, and from there we went to our new mother and new life. Maybe the past was too painful for anyone to talk about and so it was relegated to oblivion, apart from those mysterious annual visits to Silcoates Lane.

Why I did not settle peacefully into this arrangement was a puzzle to me until I began to piece together my real history. I was always a great reader, a loner by circumstance, not choice. There were so many contradictory sides to my character. I longed desperately for a mother's love and care, which I seemed to see my half sister getting, and yet I could put no words on my yearning.

Then one day, leafing through some copies of Arthur Mee's *Children's Encyclopedia,* I came upon a copy of a painting that depicted Ruth and Naomi at the crossing of the river before Bethlehem. I don't know who the artist was, nor have I ever come across that painting since, but it spoke to me in a unique way. There were two women, one older, one younger, who obviously loved one another and were going to go on together. This was a picture of female mother-daughter bonding that was missing in my own life. I wanted to experience what I had been denied. I wanted to meet and know women of integrity such as I felt my mother must have been. I was awed at her courage in choosing a new life, when society would have demanded death rather than divorce. I admired her confidence when I had none of my own.

So began the journey that would take me into religious life, where I would meet many women of courage and spirit, but many others who were content with a routine, undemanding existence. I met women who were servants and women who were queens in their small world. Many times I relived the story of Ruth, wanting to travel on with those who seemed older and more experienced than me, seeing them as worthy role models. But I clung to others who were themselves clinging for safety to the past and to known security, rather than traveling into a future that beckoned but which was still unsure.

The story of Ruth has spoken to my heart powerfully of growth and courage and willingness to move on; just as at other times it has spoken of the need for a place and home before one can reach out to others. But always this story has been lived in the context of relationships. Only now am I beginning to know from experience that the story of Ruth culminates in her own independence, her own ability to relate as an individual, to claim her own being and so become fruitful through her union with Boaz. I am no longer Ruth looking for a Naomi to "mother" me and accompany me; I am no longer seeking someone to validate me. I am my own Naomi, who brings along the inner Ruth and invites her to a new and untried life of dedication in a new land.

The Hebrew Scriptures take human history seriously. It is through the preservation of oral stories that the Jewish people came to understand both their God and their God's action in the world. Story is the remembered past—remembered and retold because it is significant for the present.

The Bible is basically a collection of stories, woven into cyclic patterns that tell of patriarchs and their wives, of kings and prophets, of great men and women who left their mark, whether for good or evil, on Israel's history. The writers of the sacred text recreate them in vivid tales of proclamation, progeny, war, conquest, exodus and exile. God is *within* human life and its attendant emotions and experiences, not somewhere else "out there." God, the Lord of events, is present in history as it unfolds. God is present to God's people in their story, in ways we can recognize, in ways with which we can identify.

Ruth is one such story. It is not a once-for-all account belonging only to the distant past. It is a story lived out in the lives of many women and men at ever deeper levels, in various ways at differing periods of life, and in different periods of history. It is a story of a bride and her widowhood, journey and place, bereavement and new birth, death and resurrection. It is a story related to our own past, present and future.

Ruth shows us God at work in the daily life and experience of one particular family through its womenfolk, whereas most of the Old Testament recounts stories of men: their military exploits, their calling to leadership, their words of prophecy, their immersion in politics and the great events of Israel's history. In the book of Ruth, we see life from the perspective of two women who work out the theme of God's loving-kindness in scenes which challenge us to find God within the circumstances of our own daily lives. "I no longer attempt to hide from myself that I think love, human personal love, is the root of all that is good," wrote Caryll Houselander. The story of Ruth upholds this insight.

Why were Ruth and Naomi remembered? Why has their story been included in the canon of Scripture? Some say it comes from the period following the Babylonian exile, that it is a tale to encourage the returning Jews to accept the foreigners in their midst and not despise intermarriage—the great King David had himself had a Moabite foremother. Others place the story earlier, suggesting it is a simple account of domestic piety set in the period of the Judges when relationships between the tribal peoples of the near East were still fluid.

However the story originated, it now stands in the Christian Bible (and in the Jewish Septuagint) between Judges and 1 Samuel, in what seems to be logical historical order. In the Hebrew Scriptures it retains its traditional place among the Writings or *Meggiloth*, five short books that belong to various feasts of the Jewish liturgical year.

Ruth is the book assigned to Pentecost, the feast when the giving of the Law on Sinai is commemorated in story and song.

The earliest festivals in the Jewish calendar were harvest festivals. The Israelites had settled on the fringe of the fertile crescent and therefore had three harvests to celebrate each year. The first was the barley harvest, followed some two months later by the gathering of the first fruits: grapes, figs, pomegranates, olives and dates, which ripened at the same time as the wheat. Finally in the autumn came the feast of ingathering, equivalent to our "harvest home," when the vines were stripped and wine put aside for fermentation. Upon these early celebrations were imposed the pattern of feasts commemorating salvation history: Passover, Pentecost and Tabernacles.

Passover, which commemorated the deliverance of the Israelites from slavery in Egypt, was the spring festival at which we find Ruth returning to Bethlehem "at the beginning of the barley harvest." When the temple was built, a sheaf of barley was ceremoniously "waved before the Lord" on the second day of Passover. It was, and still is, a time for reading the Song of Songs, that dialogue of springtime love between God and his people, mirrored in human sexual love and the delight man and woman take in one another.

Forty-nine days were counted from this offering of a barley sheaf, and on the fiftieth day, Pentecost, the feast of the first fruits was kept. A basket of fresh produce was taken to the temple by each worshiper and laid before the presiding priest with a declaration of gratitude for the people's deliverance from Egypt. The basket held fruit gathered from the land "flowing with milk and honey" that had been God's gift. This tradition survives now only in the decoration of the synagogue with flowers and fruit at this time.

The third agricultural festival, Tabernacles, coincided with the full harvest moon. It was customary to erect a form of temporary shelter or booth in the garden, or on a balcony or roof, in which to take some meals and to sing joyful hymns of praise and thanksgiving.

Just as the celebration of harvest is built into the very structure of the natural order, so the Israelites came to celebrate God's power and care in the events of their national and personal histories.

The feast of Pentecost, on which the book of Ruth is read in its entirety, revolves around the gift of the Law to Israel and the blessings that accrue to the people through this gift. It is celebrated in an agricultural setting, for Ruth marries Boaz at the end of harvest time, just as she comes to Bethlehem at the beginning of barley harvest.

But there is more to the book of Ruth than a pastoral idyll. Ruth is a story of human love and devotion unsurpassed in any literature and it has universal religious implications. Ruth was a Moabite—the daughter of a people reckoned among Israel's bitterest enemies. She is a figure of the Gentiles who are summoned to join Israel, an ancestor of the Messiah through her great-grandson David.

On the surface, the theme of the book of Ruth is a simple tale of a girl who leaves home to align herself with God's people. God and God's action are not explicitly mentioned. God does not intrude but is present as the story unfolds, and providence asserts itself in and through familiar happenings. The Divine Presence is intuited rather than explicit. God is the one who blesses and validates human choices when they are made with integrity. God works in and through the social customs of the period and the relationships that evolve in the process.

Ruth is, in fact, a story of death and resurrection, repentance and redemption, set in a feminine idiom. It is a story for everyone. And it is a story for now.

PART ONE

Chapter One

SETTING THE SCENE

¹ In the days when the judges ruled, there was a famine in the land, and a certain man of Bethlehem in Judah went to live in the country of Moab, he and his wife and two sons. ² The name of the man was Elimelech and the name of his wife Naomi, and the names of his two sons were Mahlon and Chilion; they were Ephrathites from Bethlehem in Judah. They went into the country of Moab and remained there.

The first chapter of the book of Ruth encompasses two journeys, a journey away from and back to Bethlehem in Judea.

Bethlehem—what town awakens more emotions for the Christian than this one, apart maybe from Jerusalem? The houses that stand have stood for over three millennia. Bethlehem is inextricably linked with the cards and pictures of Christmas, redolent with the imagery we conceived as children when the snow lay on the ground and we sang "O, Little Town of Bethlehem" thinking of the shepherds in frosty fields listening to the glad tidings of the angels' song. There in a manger filled with straw lay a tiny infant, his mother in a blue robe beside him, lost in adoration, with Joseph standing watchfully by. Through the starry night shepherds and kings wended their way to this shadowy abode, softly illumined by the haloes of the Holy Family.

Later, the great art of the West may have modified our image of the scene: Rembrandt's Dutch barn with its peasants in attendance, Raphael's Madonnas in flowing gowns, the glory of Botticelli's angels dancing over the stable. Christmas is forever being relived and revisioned in contemporary terms, but the magic of childhood never totally leaves it.

Bethlehem is about twenty miles south of Jerusalem. It is an Arab Christian city in the main, its streets narrow, the air alive with the sound of bells that chime the beginning of services in the various churches, convents and monasteries of the area. Dominating all, the great Church of the Nativity ushers worshippers into its dark interior, the entrance door so low one has to bend to enter it. Tradition says it was constructed so on purpose, in order to prevent Muslim horsemen riding in and causing havoc among the congregation when the East was under the dominion of the Ottoman Empire. Massive pillars of dull red stone support the roof and divide the interior of the basilica into nave and aisles. The building dates from the era of Constantine and is the earliest Christian church still in use. King Edward IV of England himself sent a gift of English oaks to reconstruct its roof, transporting them with tons of lead via the republic of Venice to Jaffa. There, Franciscan friars, who have long had custody of the holy places, took charge of the precious gift and conveyed it on the last leg of its journey to Bethlehem.

The church is constructed above the cave that tradition recognizes as the birthplace of Christ. It is accessed by flights of steps which lead beneath the high altar, and the cave's interior is lit by silver lamps that gleam amid clouds of incense in the darkness. So sacred is this place, marked by a star around which words proclaim "Here Jesus Christ was born of the Virgin Mary," that the star's removal led to a quarrel between France and Russia that blazed into the Crimean War.

Bethlehem has stood through waves of conquest: Jews, Romans, Arabs, European Crusaders, Saracens, Turks. The Crusader style of dress is still evident in the national costume of the Arab women of Bethlehem. It consists of a high headdress with a flowing veil pinned under the chin, worn with a long dress, beautifully embroidered and enhanced with silver thread where possible.

Around Bethlehem are a number of old houses built over limestone caves. It was presumably in such a one as this that Jesus was born that first Christmas night. The single living room is reached by a flight of stone steps, the animals being stalled on the ground level. These feed from rude mangers cut into the rock.

As one approaches the town today, one sees white houses clinging to the hillside; they shimmer in the heat, while lizards dart in and out of the stone walls. Vines and fig trees display their fruit under the hot sun, while all around the fields of wheat and barley ripen in season.

On its east side, Bethlehem is close to the Judean desert, and the road drops off into a gorge that leads toward the Dead Sea and its strange salt shapes, recalling the living death of Lot's wife. In the distance, the mountains of Moab, streaked with purple and mauve shadows, slash the skyline.

Bethlehem is already mentioned in the Book of Genesis. It was on the road just outside the earliest settlement that Rachel, beloved wife of the patriarch Jacob, died in childbirth. It was her second child, following the long wait for her firstborn Joseph after years of barrenness. The mother lingered long enough to be assured of her infant's safe arrival, and named him Benoni ("son of my sorrow") with her dying breath. Jacob, however, renamed him Benjamin ("son of the south"). In memory of Rachel, Jacob erected a pillar at her grave.[1] This tomb is now a sacred site where Jewish, Christian and Muslim women still go to pray for fertility and a safe labor.

Bethlehem was, is and always will be the "town of mother and child." The book of Ruth, too, culminates in a birth, another mother and child, with a very happy grandmother completing the picture.

After the exodus, when the Israelites parceled out the land of Canaan, the south was given to the tribes of Benjamin and Judah. But in the time of the Judges there was little stability and frequent skirmishes among warring clans were commonplace. Farmers would find their crops ruined by raiders, or destroyed by drought. The hot wind blowing from the nearby desert could keep rain at bay for years at a time. For subsistence farmers, a year or two of tragedy could mean the difference between life and death for whole families and even whole villages.

It was in one of these famines that a Bethlehem family, comprising husband, wife and two sons (Elimelech, Naomi, Mahlon and Chilion), journeyed to Moab to seek sustenance. As has been said, the mountains of Moab are visible on the horizon from Bethlehem and are but a few days' journey away. The group may have settled in Moab proper, the rolling plains of the plateau east of the Dead Sea, but it is more likely that they remained in the foothills and plains to the northeast, which were irrigated by little watercourses meandering through the shallow valleys.

Moab was the country in which Lot had taken refuge after the destruction of Sodom, and his daughters, through their incestuous relationship with their father, were considered the ancestors of the Ammonites and Moabites.[2] Those two women grasped the only opportunity they had for progeny and proved fruitful against the odds. In Ruth, we find echoes of those earlier "strong women," and witness the redemption of the Moabite people through the love bestowed on an Israelite woman by a Moabite daughter-in-law who cherished her.

It seems probable that, during the period spoken of in the book of Ruth, some of the area around Moab had recently been deserted, leaving land free for possession by wandering tribespeople.

The book of Judges recounts how Eglon, a Moabite chieftain, had ravaged the whole of southern Canaan, setting up his principle fortress in Jericho, city of palm trees, and from there exacting tribute from the Benjaminites of Judea whom he kept in subjection.[3]

Eventually, a man appointed to bear the required tribute to Eglon formed a brave plan to assassinate the tyrant. His name was Ehud, and he put his idea into execution single-handedly (the term is intentional, as it was due to Ehud's left-handedness that the ruse succeeded). Having delivered the tribute to Eglon, a grossly fat potentate, Ehud departed, traveling as far as Gilgal. There he left his companions and turned back alone.

Presumably, in the search that had preceded the first visit it was ascertained that Ehud carried no weapon on his left side where a dagger would usually be secreted. Meanwhile, declaring that he had a private oracle to impart to Eglon, Ehud obtained a private audience in the upper chamber of the fortress.

Once there, with the door closed behind them, Ehud repeated that he bore a special message, rose from his seat and, taking the two-sided dagger from beside his right thigh, thrust it into Eglon's belly. The man was so obese that the chronicler delights in recounting that the dagger went in smoothly up to the hilt, the flesh closing over the blade, while the dirt from his intestines gushed over the floor. Quickly securing the inside bolt, Ehud made his way down the outer staircase and escaped.

Time passed. The attendants returned and found the door locked; so they waited, thinking their chief must have wanted privacy to relieve himself. More time passed and they became suspicious. At length, they forced the door, only to find their lord slain and his attacker far away. In the chaos that followed, Ehud managed to rout the Moabites and eject them from their strongholds, pushing them back over the Jordan and away from Benjamin and Judah. But the resulting upheaval could well have left good farmland deserted, ready for victorious Israelites to move in and take advantage of the fertile fields.

So the book of Ruth begins with an account of one family's decision to move to Moab. They left behind them all that was familiar in order to make a new life for themselves in a foreign land. If they had not done so, the story of Ruth would never have been told, and the Messiah would have had a different genealogy.

In each of our lives there is a chain of seemingly arbitrary circumstances that we can only interpret in retrospect. If my mother had not traveled to India, she would never have met my father. If his first wife had not died, he would not have been free to marry another woman, and so the particular children who were my brother and I would never have been born. If my mother had not died in her turn, we would never have gone to Jersey, nor would the mystery of 44 Silcoates Lane have ever puzzled us.

In every life there are areas of "what if." Only much later can we discern the providence of God in everything and praise the Divine wisdom. But that, of course, depends on our acceptance of life, of our own particular life, and, as circumstances present themselves, making the choices that events seem to demand.

LORD,

give me the wisdom
to accept all that has made my life what it is.
May I accept the past
with its attendant circumstances,
and find in it matter to praise you
for your providence and tender care.
And when I do not understand,
help me to trust that wherever I am,
and wherever I have been,
you are present, too.
You are working out your purposes
in the great web of human relationships
whereby we are bonded one to another.
Lord, this I believe;
help my unbelief.

Notes

[1] Genesis 35:16–20.
[2] Genesis 19:30–38.
[3] Judges 3:12–30.

Chapter Two

BEREAVEMENT

> ³ *But Elimelech, the husband of Naomi, died, and she was left with her two sons. ⁴ These took Moabite wives; the name of the one was Orpah and the name of the other Ruth. When they had lived there about ten years, ⁵ both Mahlon and Chilion also died, so that the woman was left without her two sons and her husband.*
>
> > ⁶ *Then she started to return with her daughters-in-law from the country of Moab, for she had heard in the country of Moab that the LORD had considered his people and given them food. ⁷ So she set out from the place where she had been living, she and her two daughters-in-law, and they went on their way to go back to the land of Judah.*

The names of the protagonists in this story are worth looking at. *Elimelech* possibly means "my God is king," *Naomi* "pleasant" or "delightful," *Chilion* and *Mahlon* respectively "little" and "sickly," so that the reader is subtly alerted to the fact that these lads will not surmount hardships easily. *Orpah* (who, we learn later, must be the name of the wife of Chilion) seems to mean "back of the neck," perhaps a reference to her turning back. The name *Ruth* is even more obscure in its etymology but probably means "refreshment." The storyteller may have had a double purpose in mind—to prepare his listeners/readers for approaching catastrophe among the menfolk (the man who should have taken the Lord as King has left the Promised Land, his two sons are physically weak), while trying to preserve historical accuracy as well. There is no reason why these names might not have been real names, and every evidence suggests that they actually were. But with the two lads and Orpah, the names might have been fictionalized because the real names were forgotten or unrecorded.

All the hopefulness attendant on that first journey to Moab was soon eroded. Loss of native land was followed by loss of the head of the family. In the effort to keep the family name alive the sons took Moabite wives. What had at first been intended as a brief sojourn in Moab had turned into a settled residence. But the sons were not strong. The promise of grandchildren receded as the young men weakened, and within ten years Naomi was left a childless widow with two foreign daughters-in-law dependent upon her.

It must have been a bitter enough experience for Naomi to see her two sons "marry out." It was only natural that they should seek wives from among the native population, girls who needed husbands and were willing to align themselves with the foreigners in their midst. These brides would be unfamiliar with Naomi's religion, worshippers of the god Chemosh. They were not part of the chosen people, inheritors of the promise, heirs of the covenant. Children born to them might be brought up practicing a synthetic religion that compromised the worship of the true God of Israel. But they were childless. Interestingly, they are not called "barren," a term which subtly blames the woman for sterility. Here the inference is that the husbands were unable to provide them with offspring.

From this point, the women dominate the story. They are the "survivors"; they must make decisions for themselves, though the position of widows in the ancient world was desperate. Without the protection of a husband or strong male relative they had to rely on charity; they had no place in society. They were marginal people, vulnerable to exploitation, without status and without honor. The first youth of all three was over, their hearts were bereft, and their bodies were no longer virginal. Who would want them now?

Naomi then makes the only decision she feels able to make in such a situation. She hears that there is food available once more in her own land and she prepares to return, taking her daughters-in-law with her. They are all she has. They will be company for one another. So Naomi sets out, returning to Judah.

There are in the first chapter of Ruth eleven appearances in one form or another of words based on the Hebrew root *lashuv*, "to return." *Teshuva*, "repentance" or "return," is not a single event but a process. Naomi turns toward God and that journey requires many acts of turning along the way. The journey recalls the parable of the prodigal son who returns to his father after a sojourn in a far-off land. He has become sick of a life of independence, of doing his own will rather than his father's. So he journeys homeward. He returns to the father.

Naomi, Ruth and Orpah are at the beginning of a journey. They know what they are leaving; they do not yet know what awaits them. We never return to life as it has been. Even if Naomi once knew the land of Judah, she had been away for ten years. People would have grown older as she herself had. There would be marriages she had not witnessed, children who had been born in her absence. Bethlehem would be different; she would be the outsider coming back, not one who had remained there through the difficult years of famine to the present prosperity.

So Naomi leaves Moab. She seizes upon a process that affirms life and hope. She moves toward redemption. But it is a slow process that still has many unknown twists to it. Within a few moments, Naomi will even be having second thoughts about taking along those who now accompany her.

For us, too, there are many times in life when we seek to return—to God, to our heritage, to family and friends—when we have been far away. It isn't just a matter of human resolve but of grace, an invitation to be accepted or refused. If we have committed ourselves once, it is harder to risk another commitment. It may mean admitting a mistake, a wrong choice, coming back not knowing how or whether we will be welcomed. And yet, because of the assurance of the words of Jesus, we are able to trust that in repentance and return a welcome awaits us.

I like to think of Mary as a Naomi figure. She attracted me to Catholicism as a teenager. She is the older woman who teaches the way of the Lord, who initiates us into the meaning and mystery of being a woman belonging to God's people. Like the relationship between Naomi and Ruth it is a relationship of friendship that crosses boundaries of age and culture.

Like Ruth in her first marriage, I committed myself to religious life when I was young and virginal. But circumstances changed and I knew I had to move to another order, move to the "land of Carmel," which I felt was my true home. It was a difficult decision and a dark journey. I knew, too, that the order that would receive me was not getting a person who was "unspoiled" and "unformed." I was prepared for suspicion and difficulties (although these did not materialize). But whatever lay ahead, I knew that I must go on and follow my intuition that another place and other companions would be right for me, without denying the past and all I had received from it. Like Ruth and Naomi, I had to learn how to integrate the past without returning to it. It is always time, whether our decisions are big or small, to enter the process of repentance and return.

LORD,

teach me the true meaning of repentance.
May I never be afraid to return to you with trust
and with a heart full of hope.
Bless those who have been my companions
at each step of the way,
those who have shared my life
and challenged me to grow.
Let me thank you for everything,
but most especially for being a God who forgives
and who promises healing and new life.
Mary, be my companion
and my friend on all my journeys.

Chapter Three

Naomi Offers a Choice

⁸ But Naomi said to her two daughters-in-law, "Go back each of you to your mother's house. May the LORD deal kindly with you, as you have dealt with the dead and with me. ⁹ The LORD grant that you may find security, each of you in the house of your husband." Then she kissed them, and they wept aloud. ¹⁰ They said to her, "No, we will return with you to your people." ¹¹ But Naomi said, "Turn back, my daughters, why will you go with me? Do I still have sons in my womb that they may become your husbands? ¹² Turn back, my daughters, go your way, for I am too old to have a husband. Even if I thought there was hope for me, even if I should have a husband tonight and bear sons, ¹³ would you then wait until they were grown? Would you then refrain from marrying? No, my daughters, it has been far more bitter for me than for you, because the hand of the LORD has turned against me."

Along the way Naomi suddenly seems to change her mind. The three women halt, and Naomi explains the situation to those she loves and terms her "daughters," so close have they become to her.

Does she have second thoughts about going back to Bethlehem with two dependent women in tow? Maybe, like many in midlife, she wants to make a fresh beginning unhampered by the past. She had thought she wanted company, now she looks at the other side of the coin. She prefers her independence, even in poverty, and anyway, she cannot offer anything to Orpah and Ruth. She can promise no security, no children, and a home and husband mean so much. Why should her daughters-in-law jeopardize their chances of motherhood to stay with someone who cannot give them what they must want before all else?

Naomi refers them to the Hebrew law of levirate, by which, when a man died, it was incumbent on his brother to marry the widow. The first son born of this union would then carry on the name and inherit the land of the deceased.

The most famous case of this nature is recounted in the book of Genesis and is referred to later in the story of Ruth. It is the case of Tamar (Genesis 38:1–30).

Tamar had been married to Judah's son Er, then, when he died, to Judah's second son Onan. Onan, too, died as a result of refusing to raise heirs to his brother. Judah then sent Tamar back to her parents, promising that when his third son, Shelah, had reached adulthood, she would be wedded to him.

But Judah did not keep his promise. Shelah attained manhood, yet remained single, and Tamar saw her chances of children receding.

In desperation, Tamar disguised herself as a prostitute. She veiled her face and sat by the road when she knew Judah would be passing that way. Judah fell into the trap and had sexual relations with her, not realizing the woman was his daughter-in-law. As he had nothing with which to pay for her favors, he promised to send a kid from his flock later, and in pledge gave her his signet, cord and staff. But when he had a friend deliver the kid, the woman could not be found and no one seemed to know of any harlot who frequented that place. Judah had to resign himself to letting her keep the pledges. He had tried to honor his word and he did not want people to laugh at him for his gullibility.

Three months later, word reaches Judah that Tamar is pregnant. As the head of the family, he reacts with fury.

She must have committed adultery. She is to be brought out and burned.

As Tamar is being led to her death, she cunningly sends word to her father-in-law that the man whose signet, cord and staff she sends him is father of the child within her womb.

Judah then is forced to acknowledge his failure to fulfill the levirate law by denying Tamar his third son Shelah. She is in the right and he in the wrong. She has grasped her opportunity in the only way she knew how. Judah, not Tamar, is the one who bears the blame. The twins she delivers when her time has come are Perez and Zerah, Perez being an ancestor of Boaz, who we meet later in the story of Ruth.

Naomi, conscious of the levirate law, tries to persuade Ruth and Orpah that it would be useless for them to expect her to bear further sons who could be their husbands in some far-off future. She is old. The situation is laughable. Even if she could find herself a husband and conceive that very night, the women would have reached menopause before the boys were grown! Better to turn back now while there is still time—time to find a man to cherish them and give them children and a secure place in society. Meanwhile, let them return to their mothers. Let them take what joy they can. Naomi will go her way, hugging to herself her bitterness at the Lord's dealings with her.

It is interesting that Naomi urges Orpah and Ruth to return to their mothers' houses, rather than their fathers' houses, which would be the usual expression. Judah sends Tamar back to her "father's house." This is another indication that the mother-bond is important in this story, as well as friendship and love between the sexes. To whom do the younger women feel closest—their own mothers or Naomi? Depending on the answer they give, they will choose the way of life of the Moabites or of the Jews. It is the mother who has the most influence over the daughter when it comes to choices that matter.

It is interesting, too, to speculate on why Naomi brings in the argument she does at the point that she does. The levirite law was surely not something that suddenly occurred to her on the way to Bethlehem. She had known of it before she set out. Either she had been ignoring the implications for Orpah and Ruth or it suddenly struck her what it might mean for them in practice. Or, as suggested, she might merely have wanted her independence and not to have to face her past acquaintances saddled with two more mouths to feed.

Saint Teresa of Avila says that the reasons we find ridiculous and disregard when we do not want to do something are the very reasons that strike us as utterly compelling when we want to do the very same thing.[1] How true!

Is Naomi, then, invoking the law because she has decided she wants her freedom? Is she allowing common sense to prevail over accepted custom? Or is she genuinely trying to redeem her bitterness and anger by an act of charity, considering the true good of others (as she sees it) before her own?

There is no one persuasive explanation. Why we do something makes all the difference. The outward act may be the same. The interior disposition shows whether we act from selflessness or self-regard, whether the other person, or merely our own desires, is important. We can gloss over nearly anything by quoting a rule to justify our actions.

Living as a religious sister, a priest, a Christian, a parishioner, there are bound to be customs and rules that impinge on my freedom. How do I view these? Do I use them only when they are to my advantage? Do I quote them to avoid sacrificial action or the responsibility of choice? In this area, I can never pass judgment on others. I can only examine my own motives and pray for light.

Lord,

help me to act from the right motives
and not presume to judge the motives of others.
Let me not act from bitterness and despair,
but with a real desire that others
may be free to choose,
even when their choice costs me dearly.
Help me to see what rules are important
and which are mere human customs.
May your love inspire my actions
and may your Spirit enlighten my heart
as I seek to do your will.

Notes

[1] Teresa of Avila, *Foundations, Collected Works*, vol. III, E. Allison Peers, trans. (London: Sheed & Ward, 1972), p. 23.

Chapter Four

THE CHOICE IS MADE

> [14] *Then they wept aloud again. Orpah kissed her*
> *mother-in-law, but Ruth clung to her.*
>
> > [15] *So she said, "See, your sister-in-law has gone*
> *back to her people and to her gods; return after your*
> *sister-in-law."* [16] *But Ruth said,*
> > *"Do not press me to leave you*
> > > *or to turn back from following you!*
> > *Where you go, I will go;*
> > > *where you lodge I will lodge;*
> > *your people shall be my people,*
> > > *and your God my God.*
> > [17] *Where you die, I will die—*
> > > *there will I be buried.*
> > *May the* LORD *do thus and so to me,*
> > > *and more as well,*
> > *if even death parts me from you!"*
> [18] *When Naomi saw that she was determined to go with*
> *her, she said no more to her.*

Ruth's words to Naomi are rightly famous. They have echoed down through the centuries and become a model for human response, not just to other humans but to the Divine as well. "Let us go both together, Lord," wrote Teresa of Avila; "Wherever you go I will go, and by whatever way you pass I will follow."[1] Ruth's words have been adopted by the Marriage Encounter Movement in which couples pledge their love to each other until death.

Orpah takes the sensible option and turns back. Why go with Naomi and choose her God when that God has brought Naomi such sorrow? Why go to a strange land when what is familiar is close by? Orpah's departure reflects her empathy for Naomi's pain. She realizes that her mother-in-law does not want her, and she decides not to burden her further. Orpah's return to Moab was not the original plan. She wanted to go with Naomi and she leaves her with tears; her story will now be separate from those with whom she has shared much of her life so far.

Ruth, however, stays on. She chooses Naomi and an unknown destiny. She chooses Naomi's God in a fidelity that will last to death. She chooses the way of life of the Hebrew people in contrast to the way of the Moabites. She chooses her mother-in-law before her own mother and the companionship of Orpah.

At various crisis points of life we, too, have to make difficult decisions. Shall I go or stay? Shall I throw in my lot with this person or this community? Whatever is chosen or not chosen is a step in the dark, but we must, like Ruth, bring to it all we have and have become so far. The past cannot be changed. Ruth will always be a woman who had been married to an Israelite and then widowed, a woman who had had specific experiences, who came from a certain time and place and scene. She could not negate the past, but she could choose to redefine it, give it new meaning through choices made in the present.

Ruth is here the female equivalent of Abraham. She is not called directly by God, but by the circumstances of her life and the pull of human love. She travels to a new land where her destiny will be revealed to her.

Jesus called people to follow him, to go with him. We are summoned to choose discipleship in response to that call, to be ready to leave all else in order to make his people ours, his God ours. We have to let him take us wherever he wants, pledging ourselves to follow without any guarantee except his love, his fidelity, his word. But for most of us there is no divine voice to direct us. It is with human limitations and within human circumstances that our choices are made.

For Ruth the past is barren; the future holds the promise of fruitfulness, although she does not yet know it. Her first marriage linked her to Naomi. Her second marriage will make her fruitful for Naomi and bring her joy.

The Lord called Abraham to "Go from your country and your kindred and your father's house to the land that I will show you. I will make of you a great nation, and I will bless you, and make your name great, so that you will be a blessing" (Genesis 12:1–2).

Abraham is called to be a blessing not just for himself but for others. He is called before the covenant is sealed. He goes forth in trust.

Any vocation is not for self alone. It is for others, also. It is to recognize that we are blessed and are asked to be a blessing for others, just as Ruth will prove a blessing to her mother-in-law and to her new husband and child in due course. Like Abraham, she hopes that, despite the odds, her choice is the right one.

Ruth counts as a "nobody," a widow without status, without rights, except the rights of the dispossessed. Of the two women, Orpah and Ruth, Ruth is the weaker. She "clings" to Naomi, as one who is dependent on the older woman for meaning. Ruth is unable to let Naomi go because of her own human needs. Ruth cannot "go it alone" with the courage of Orpah. She is an embodied witness to the words of the Magnificat that God chooses the lowly, the weak, the powerless, for his purposes. Ruth has not yet attained real love for her mother-in-law, and certainly not for God. She clings. She needs. She has to have Naomi beside her or she will lose herself. She is ready to change her religion, to do anything at all in order to stay with Naomi. Only with time will this dependent and needy love be purified.

Love is a process. It does not happen all at once, and one cannot ask from a young person the kind of love that belongs to maturity.

One July day in high summer, I, too, made a choice. It was my solemn profession as a Carmelite. The sanctuary was filled with summer flowers—delphiniums, roses, honeysuckle. I had chosen the words of Ruth for my Scripture reading. I wanted to go with this community, to live with these people, to learn from them about a God who was still hidden from my consciousness. It may have looked to outsiders as if I was making a great sacrifice, but it seemed to cost nothing. It would have cost far more for me to leave. I felt I could not live alone without my Carmelite companions. I would cease to exist, fall into nothingness, I had so little sense of myself. As for God, I still lived in hope that somehow God would, in time, become a reality in my life. I just stuck with people who seemed to know what God was all about.

In my religious life I had seen others "turn back" like Orpah, make other choices for free, independent living. I almost envied their courage. I could not survive in the outside world. Though some imagine that vows require great strength, I embraced them because I was weak. Appearances can be very deceptive!

Ruth herself does not say, "I choose the Israelite people and their God." She makes clear that she is choosing Naomi's people and God. She is making a relational choice. It is in the context of a particular relationship that she makes her statement of faith. She wants Naomi to transcend her own pain in order to let her daughter-in-law accompany her. There must have been something in Naomi that attracted Ruth so much that she could not bear to leave her. In her weakness, Ruth chose a difficult path, but she could actually do no other. It would be for God to make her strong, so that the choice could be validated as Ruth grew to a deeper maturity and sense of her individuality.

For many, God will always be a "hidden" God, but that does not mean the Holy One is not present. God is present in the very process by which we grow to mature love, and it may well include dependency, clinging and emotional pain along the way.

LORD,

teach me to be patient

in the time it takes to learn the meaning of love.

May I be alert to discover my vocation

in and through all that happens to me.

Even if I hesitate,

don't let my resolve weaken.

Wherever you go, I want to go.

I want to live where you live.

May your people be my people

and your God my God.

Invite me day by day to go with you,

and help me to respond with a loving heart.

Notes

[1] Adapted from Teresa of Avila, *Way of Perfection, Collected Works* vol. II, E. Allison Peers, ed. and trans. (London: Sheed and Ward, 1972), p. 108.

Chapter Five

THE RETURN

> [19] *So the two of them went on until they came to Bethlehem. When they came to Bethlehem, the whole town was stirred because of them; and the women said, "Is this Naomi?"* [20] *She said to them,*
>
> "Call me no longer Naomi,
>   call me Mara,
>   for the Almighty has dealt
>   bitterly with me.
> [21]*I went away full,*
>   but the LORD has brought
>   me back empty;
> why call me Naomi
>   when the LORD has dealt
>   harshly with me,
> and the Almighty has brought
>   calamity upon me?"
>
> [22] *So Naomi returned together with Ruth the Moabite, her daughter-in-law, who came back with her from the country of Moab. They came to Bethlehem at the beginning of the barley harvest.*

And so Ruth and Naomi face the rest of the journey back to Naomi's native town. What must it have been like for Naomi to return and Ruth to see Bethlehem for the first time? Naomi sees the same houses clinging to the same hillside, just as she had left them, and the same fields, but this time ripe for harvest and no longer stricken and withered by drought. The hills of Moab recede into the distance as the two widows, tired by the long journey, lean against one another on the road. Their destination draws closer. The white houses take on more definite shapes. People are seen moving about their business.

What awaits the wanderers? Ruth has sacrificed everything an ancient Semite could—home, kindred, native religion, burial with her own people, every guarantee of protection. All she has is the woman she has begged to accompany. She will share the fate that awaits her mother-in-law, whatever it may be.

As they approach Bethlehem, the women of the town suddenly recognize the one who had departed for Moab ten years previously. But where is her husband? Where are her sons? Who is her present companion? And why is Naomi so haggard, gray and bent when she had left with a light step and a dark head of hair? Can this really be the same woman? They set up a little ceremony of welcome which allows Naomi to release her anger, and the women provide an audience to listen to her explanation.

Naomi breaks into a lament. She has to verbalize her pain, have others acknowledge the depths of her grief and bereavement. She will gloss over nothing. She does not even refer to Ruth, who has given up all to be with her. Ruth then learns one of love's first lessons: one has to bear silently being overlooked. The love of one person for another does not drive away all grief and pain in the beloved.

"Do not call me Naomi, call me Mara," says the older woman. How can her heart be so empty when Ruth's brims with love? But Ruth knows that a new balance is being struck. Naomi had been a stranger in Moab and had been accepted after a time. Ruth is now the stranger in Judah and it will take time for her to be integrated into this new group of Naomi's former friends.

Loss is one of the central themes of psychology. The experience of loss must be faced honestly, grappled with and not ignored or minimized. After her many losses

Naomi renames herself Mara (meaning "bitter"). The women who greet her allow her this renaming. Unlike Job's friends they do not try to tell her she must have deserved her fate, that it is not really so bad or that "God permits these things so as to try us." They allow her full self-expression. They give her dignity in her grief.

Naomi is here in touch with the biblical tradition that gives great importance to names. In renaming herself she is challenging God to adjust her fate so that it once more corresponds with the meaning of her original name, "Pleasant." This is the only place in the story where Naomi is called Mara. Almost immediately her name reverts to Naomi as her condition improves.

The ability to articulate and communicate experience is a source of power for these women. They need to emphasize their bonds to one another rather than dwell on their separation. Most of the women who listen to Naomi will also have known their own share of pain—death was always a close companion in the ancient world—from childbirth, disease, natural disaster, war, accident. Why pretend that all is well?

Naomi calls God to task. She is powerless, but her words, like Ruth's, have the capacity to name the truth and clarify the situation. She endows her experience with dignity through the power of the words she utters. She will not let her grief be ignored. It must be articulated and shared. Her words create and strengthen the community of the women around her. Each one may be dependent on husband or male relative under the law, but the female community exists as an option and a haven, reaffirming women's self-reliance and sense of hidden power.

All around the group the harvest is ripe, in contrast to the interior famine Naomi feels. Public acknowledgement of her private grief is essential before Naomi can move on. And so Ruth waits.

Have I the patience to allow others to grieve without rushing in with consoling words or trying to turn the conversation to more positive topics? Have I the ability to listen to another's pain and feel it with them? And have I the courage to be frank with God about what I have been through? Ruth and Naomi can teach us much as they continue the process of *teshuva*, "repentance."

LORD,

teach me to be honest in my relationships
with others and with you.
Don't let me pretend that all is well
when I am suffering loss and pain.
Rather let me trust that you
will make all well in your own time.
And may I not be afraid to call on others
to be with me and support me in my neediness
    and anguish,
just as I want to support them in my turn.

PART TWO

Chapter Six

RUTH THE GLEANER

> ¹ *Now Naomi had a kinsman on her husband's side, a prominent rich man, of the family of Elimelech, whose name was Boaz.* ² *And Ruth the Moabite said to Naomi, "Let me go to the field and glean among the ears of grain, behind someone in whose sight I may find favor." She said to her, "Go, my daughter."* ³ *So she went. She came and gleaned in the field behind the reapers. As it happened, she came to the part of the field belonging to Boaz, who was of the family of Elimelech.* ⁴ *Just then Boaz came from Bethlehem. He said to the reapers, "The LORD be with you." They answered, "The LORD bless you."* ⁵ *Then Boaz said to his servant who was in charge of the reapers, "To whom does this young woman belong?"* ⁶ *The servant who was in charge of the reapers answered, "She is the Moabite who came back with Naomi from the country of Moab.* ⁷ *She said, 'Please let me glean and gather among the sheaves behind the reapers.' So she came, and she has been on her feet from this early morning until now, without resting even for a moment."*

Ruth immediately begins to turn from her "need love" of Naomi to a growing "gift love," translated into work. She does not stay at home to enjoy Naomi's company. Instead she proves her love by moving away so as to support the pair. Work is the way she makes her love visible.

The arrival of Ruth and Naomi in Bethlehem coincided with the beginning of the spring grain harvest, a
seven-week period from about mid-April to mid-June.
Harvesting was difficult work and demanded long hours.
Young men moved through the fields carrying wooden
sickles which had sharpened pieces of flint embedded in
the blades. The sickles would be used to cut through
handfuls of grain which the binders, who followed behind
the reapers, would form into sheaves. In the course of the
work a number of stalks would fall to the ground. These
were left for poor people to "glean" or gather up to aug-
ment their meager food supply. Gleaners could, by law,
keep what they gathered in this way. The edges of the
fields, which were difficult to reach with sickles, were also
left unharvested for the poor to help themselves.

This custom had arisen because the Promised Land
was considered to be God's gift to the whole people and
not merely a favored few. Land was held in sacred trust
from generation to generation (as illustrated in the story of
Naboth, who refused to give King Ahab what he considered to be his and his ancestors' sacred portion of land, see
1 Kings 21:1–29). Landowners were obligated to employ
day laborers at a fair wage and to make provision for the
unemployed who were poor, orphaned or widowed. It
was a rudimentary form of social welfare.

> When you reap your harvest in your field and forget
> a sheaf in the field, you shall not go back to get it; it
> shall be left for the alien, the orphan and the widow,
> so that the LORD your God may bless you in all your
> undertakings. (Deuteronomy 24:19)

> When you reap the harvest of your land, you shall
> not reap to the very edges of your field, or gather the
> gleanings of your harvest. You shall not strip your
> vineyard bare, or gather the fallen grapes of your
> vineyard; you shall leave them for the poor and the
> alien: I am the LORD your God. (Leviticus 19:9–10)

As a foreigner (an "alien") Ruth was allowed to provide for her needs like the local poor. It was a compassionate law, acknowledging that the Hebrew people themselves knew what it was like to have been poor in Egypt, knew from experience how difficult it could be to exist as foreigners in a strange land. Gleaning was no light work. It meant stooping for stray stalks again and again while the hot sun beat down on the workers' backs. Naomi was either too old to join Ruth or was still nursing her grief. It fell to the Moabite girl to work for them both. An undefended woman—a foreigner, no less—would not be treated gently.

As Ruth worked her way through the fields, bending over, stretching up periodically to relieve the pain, she came to that part of the field which belonged to Boaz, a rich relative of the deceased Elimelech. Most of the fields were parceled out in unfenced strips so it was easy to pass from one part of a field to another part with different ownership.

The story of Ruth has preserved the customary greeting between reapers and owner as Boaz comes to see how the harvesting is progressing. He notices the foreign girl and in a roundabout way asks who she is, or rather "whose" she is—who is responsible for her? It is a circumlocution, since to express direct interest in a stranger was considered suspicious. The servant in charge of the reapers tells Boaz that this is the Moabite who lives with Naomi. She has asked to avail herself of a gleaner's rights and has been laboring from early morning until now without any rest.

Ruth proves industrious. She is willing to serve, to go out and claim sustenance for herself and her mother-in-law. Because she is not passive, she is open to providence, the providence that brings her to Boaz's field. Psychologist Scott Peck suggests that love is always an act of courage or work.[1] Ruth undertakes both expressions of love. It cannot have been easy to brave the stares of the native Israelites in order to work in the fields. And it was not a job for anyone gently reared. Yet Ruth worked untiringly, enough to cause others to notice and commend her.

Monastic life, to the surprise of many, places great emphasis on the need to work. In many ways it is the kind of work that Ruth is doing: not very important to outward eyes. It is gathering up the "bits and pieces" that others have overlooked, the daily service of each other within the precincts of the enclosure. Yet work is absolutly necessary for mental and spiritual health and well-being. Respect for self and respect for work are bound together. Work integrates us into the human community wherever we are.

In my own life, work has played a very important part. It has enabled me to make a contribution to life and it has taken me out of myself and a tendency to be overly concerned with my own inner workings. It has been imperative that I interact with others and wrestle with reality. The difficulty for me, if any, has been with my compulsive need to finish, to complete, to have something to show for time and effort. The energy expended in getting results can sometimes be a way of refusing to face myself, to acknowledge my poverty, and my need for the service of others.

There is also the pitfall in monasteries of thinking that what is done here—prayer—is the really important thing, rather than seeing prayer within the context of a whole life. It is perhaps easier for us to escape the challenges of earning a living, being content with only paltry effort, and using the excuse that we need to be recollected and undisturbed.

Ruth is a reminder of the backbreaking work that so many women perform to feed their families. She reminds us of the necessity for good laws and a society that provides generously for the needy. And she reminds me of God's providence that brought me to work in my own particular part of God's field, the Order of Carmel. Will

I work according to opportunities that come to me? Will I seek out as many ways to serve as possible? Or will I be content with doing the minimum because I fear risk and prefer the safety of being only with those I love, rather than behaving as a woman of God and therefore a woman who belongs to all?

LORD,

help me to value work truly.
Let me labor with a glad heart
in the field that your providence has marked
        out for me.
Whether I am called to family life
or to a career,
whether I have to experience unemployment
or the burden of overwork,
may I keep you before my eyes.
You labored at Nazareth as a carpenter.
Your mother knew the work of women
that can crush with its endless daily obligations.
May my work never blind me to human need.
Help me always to put people first,
and may what I do bear fruit for eternity.

Notes

[1] M. Scott Peck. *The Road Less Traveled* (London: Arrow Books, 1990), p. 128.

GENEROUS LOVE RECIPROCATED

> ⁸ Then Boaz said to Ruth, "Now listen, my daughter, do not glean in another field or leave this one, but keep close to my young women. ⁹ Keep your eyes on the field that is being reaped, and follow behind them. I have ordered the young men not to bother you. If you get thirsty, go to the vessels and drink from what the young men have drawn." ¹⁰ Then she fell prostrate, with her face to the ground, and said to him, "Why have I found favor in your sight, that you should take notice of me, when I am a foreigner?" ¹¹ But Boaz answered her, "All that you have done for your mother-in-law since the death of your husband has been fully told me, and how you left your father and mother and your native land and came to a people that you did not know before. ¹² May the LORD reward you for your deeds, and may you have a full reward from the LORD, the God of Israel, under whose wings you have come for refuge!" ¹³ Then she said, "May I continue to find favor in your sight, my lord, for you have comforted me and spoken kindly to your servant, even though I am not one of your servants."

Boaz is touched by Ruth's story. He invites her to continue among his women servants where she will be safe from male molestation; the women will be companions of her own age. He even instructs her to take a drink when thirsty from the common vessels provided for the paid workers, in a country where water is precious.

This whole scene is set in the context of a stable community with a culture and standards that matter. Our profound individualism is very different from the understanding that people of the ancient world had of themselves. People then existed within, and were defined by, a framework of relationships. The traditions and laws that established and governed this framework were sacred. As Ruth is initiated into these customs so she finds an ever deeper sense of personal security.

Boaz recognizes that in stepping outside her own Moabite traditions Ruth has chosen not merely Naomi but a whole way of life, including the religion in which that life is embedded and finds meaning. Her need to be assimilated into this new environment is respected and filled by Boaz's kindness toward her. His kindness is a direct result of his knowledge of Ruth's kindness to Naomi. Goodness attracts goodness.

Ruth is, therefore, the catalyst for Boaz's expression of tender concern, and she responds with deep respect. How could such a rich man take notice of a mere foreign worker? Boaz counters with the knowledge he has obtained from his chief steward. This young woman has left everything, father, mother, native country to come with her mother-in-law to a strange land.

Like Abraham and Sarah, Ruth has responded to the invitation to journey to a new land. But who commanded her to make this journey? To what voice did she respond? Her love for Naomi was its own command. Cleaving to another person in love can mean risk, stepping forth on a path one would never otherwise have taken. Only God can give a fitting reward for such conduct. Ruth has chosen the Lord in choosing Naomi and the way of life of Naomi's people; in finding refuge with Naomi, Ruth has found refuge under the Divine wings. The same Lord who dealt Naomi such a bitter hand has received a foreigner with kindness. Later in the story, we shall see how Boaz becomes a symbol of the redeeming and overshadowing love of the God Ruth has indirectly, but truly, chosen.

The reference to the wings of God may be a reference to the ark of God, which, at the time of the Judges, was still housed in a tent since the temple was not yet built. The ark was a coffer approximately five feet long, three feet wide and three feet high that had been constructed to hold the tablets of the Ten Commandments. It was covered with a plate of gold, the "mercy seat" and surmounted with winged cherubim. The ark was considered to be the glory of Israel, and the spread wings of the cherubim were symbolic of God's presence above it. As the cloud had followed the ark in the desert, so Gentiles were said to find refuge "in the shelter of the Shekinah" (meaning "the presence of God in the world").

The reference to the Lord's wings may also reflect the Deuteronomic teaching that Israel was found and cherished in the desert like an eaglet, carried upon the Lord's pinions (wings), nurtured and brought to safety.

> He sustained him [Jacob] in a desert land,
>   in a howling wilderness waste;
> he shielded him, cared for him,
>   guarded him as the apple of his eye.
> As an eagle stirs up its nest,
>   and hovers over its young;
> as it spreads its wings, takes them up
>   and bears them aloft on its pinions,
> the LORD alone guided him;
>   no foreign god was with him.
>   (Deuteronomy 32:10–12)

We all want a place where we can feel secure. There is a longing for a place to "be" when the world is in continuous motion. Perhaps this stems from an unconscious desire to return to the womb, to a time when each of us knew security and total safety, but this is not what faith is about.

The security God offers is not freedom from responsibility. God does not pour out the Divine Self in such a way that life no longer hurts us. Rather, God gives us strength to reach out to others, to give security to them and, in self-giving, reap the reward of becoming a loving, God-filled person. When the Lord shelters us, we learn to trust even amid darkness and ignorance, but we do not stop there. Judaism and Christianity both insist that we actively love our neighbor. The laws by which Ruth gleaned reflected a social consciousness ahead of its time and ahead of our own.

Ruth is a woman of action. She leaves. She works. She gives of herself. All these help her in her own personal search for the truth. The dependency and weakness she showed at the beginning of the story are being turned into strengths. Others are beginning to depend on her. Though she is unaware of it, her behavior is becoming a beacon of light for others. It is very likely that she stills *feels* helpless. But, by doing what she can, she is coming closer to the God whose providence has never left her. It is by our ordinary human lives that we grow to spiritual maturity. Ruth is developing a confidence commensurate with her courage.

Boaz's words to Ruth are the words I chose to have on my Silver Jubilee card: "May you be blessed by the Lord, the God of Israel, beneath whose sheltering wings you have learned to trust." More than twenty-five years of religious life have shown me how reliable the love of God is. But the learning can take a lifetime!

LORD,

may I find shelter beneath your wings.
May the security I feel in you
enable me to reach out to others
in word and action.
May kindness breed kindness
in my own life
and in the lives of those around me.
Make me receptive to good example.
And let me find ways to be courageous
in reaching out
to make your providence known
by my manner of living.

Chapter Eight

FOOD IN ABUNDANCE

¹⁴ At mealtime Boaz said to her, "Come here, and eat some of this bread, and dip your morsel in the sour wine." So she sat beside the reapers, and he heaped up for her some parched grain. She ate until she was satisfied, and she had some left over. ¹⁵ When she got up to glean, Boaz instructed his young men, "Let her glean even among the standing sheaves, and do not reproach her. ¹⁶ You must also pull out some handfuls for her from the bundles, and leave them for her to glean, and do not rebuke her."

¹⁷ So she gleaned in the field until evening. Then she beat out what she had gleaned, and it was about an ephah of barley. ¹⁸ She picked it up and came into the town, and her mother-in-law saw how much she had gleaned. Then she took out and gave her what was left over after she herself had been satisfied.

Boaz has not only noticed Ruth and inquired after her. He proceeds to treat her with a special affection. When it comes to the time of midday rest he calls her to join his workers, offering her bread and sour wine for refreshment—vinegar, a by-product of wine-making, was an effective thirst quencher. The parched grains of barley which he added personally were kernels roasted on an iron plate, such as Abigail took as part of the field rations to David and his men (1 Samuel 25:18). Ruth is not only fed, but she has more than is needed to satiate her appetite. What is left over she hides away to give Naomi when the day's work is over. After the meal, Boaz instructs the reapers to be especially generous with this Moabite girl, letting her glean among the standing sheaves and dropping handfuls of barley on purpose so that her work will be less arduous and more abundantly rewarded.

No wonder that when Ruth returns to Naomi in the evening Naomi can hardly believe her good fortune.

For the Christian, this part of the story of Ruth resonates with Eucharistic symbols and offers an even clearer identification of Boaz with Jesus, which will be sustained and enhanced in the next chapter.

Boaz enters into relationship with Ruth, but he is not a patriarch in the usual mode. In his wholeness he mirrors the God who is both masculine and feminine.

Ruth comes to the protecting presence of Boaz as one who is cared for by Israel's God, one who is "overshadowed by the Divine wings" (a feminine symbol).

> They shall live again beneath my shadow,
>   they shall flourish as a garden;
> they shall blossom like the vine,
>   their fragrance shall be like the wine of Lebanon.
>
> O Ephraim, what have I to do with idols?
>   It is I who answer and look after you.
> I am like an evergreen cypress;
>   your faithfulness comes from me. (Hosea 14:7–8)

Boaz is a Christ-figure. He cares; he is compassionate. He feeds as a mother feeds, and as Jesus feeds with the gift of his own Body and Blood under the appearance of bread and wine in the Eucharist.

"The mother can give her child to suck of her milk, but our precious mother Jesus, can feed us with himself, and does so most contentedly and most tenderly with the Blessed Sacrament, which is the precious food of true life."[1]

There is food provided in abundance by Boaz, with some left over, even as Jesus feeds the multitude by the Lake of Galilee, and the disciples are able to gather up baskets full of scraps.

In eating with Ruth, Boaz shares himself through food on a level of equality, even though socially there is no comparison between the status of a wealthy older man and a young foreign widow. It is because we can already sense the love behind Boaz's behavior that we can appreciate his kindness as more than condescension.

> With great delight I sat in his shadow,
>   and his fruit was sweet to my taste.
> He brought me to the banqueting house,
>   and his intention toward me was love.
>   (Song of Songs 2:3b–4)

Boaz is also an image of the Spirit who broods over chaos in order to bring from it harmony and the beauty of order, as Boaz harmonizes the work of Ruth and reapers. Here is a growing respect, a calling forth to life in the mutual honoring of all. It is an echo of what Julian of Norwich terms the "supreme friendliness of God."[2]

Equality in friendship can be true and deep despite social barriers. Jonathan, a king's son, loved David the shepherd boy; my father, an Army officer, loved a woman from another class. What matters is that one is ready to take risks and make choices on account of the other. But it can also involve conflicting loyalties and so has the potential for tragedy. The relationship of Ruth with Boaz, as of Ruth with Naomi, does not exist in a social vacuum, it is part of a larger picture. Society can either aid or hinder its development. How many splendid potential friendships have foundered on the rocks of social convention. It takes a strong person to listen to more than the opinions of others who are only too swift to counsel caution. Even loving God is a risky business!

The sharing of Holy Communion within the Christian community, with friends around me, is something I have done daily for many years. How easy it is to take it for granted, to accept this "daily bread" as if it were my due and not remember continually that it is a sign of the goodness and kindness of Jesus, the God who invites me to eat

with him and of him. There are so many places in the
world where Mass is a rarity, where the Eucharist can
be celebrated only once every few months, or even years,
because of the shortage of ordained ministers, yet I
partake daily.

And there is the question of whether I have the aware-
ness to see the many ways in which God comes to me
through the kindness of those with whom I live, those
who prepare my meals, those who ensure my well-being
in a thousand ways.

LORD,

teach me to be grateful
for the gift of Holy Communion.
Teach me to be grateful for the love
that comes to me through those around me.
And make me willing to share
what I have been given
with a generous and loving heart.

Notes

[1] Julian of Norwich, *Revelations of Divine Love*, Josef Pichler, M.H.M,
trans. (unpublished), Chapter 60.

[2] *Ibid.*, Chapter 5.

Chapter Nine

THE TIME IT TAKES

> [19] *Her mother-in-law said to her, "Where did you glean today? And where have you worked? Blessed be the man who took notice of you." So she told her mother-in-law with whom she had worked, and said, "The name of the man with whom I worked today is Boaz."* [20] *Then Naomi said to her daughter-in-law, "Blessed be he by the* LORD, *whose kindness has not forsaken the living or the dead!" Naomi also said to her, "The man is a relative of ours, one of our nearest kin."* [21] *Then Ruth the Moabite said, "He even said to me, 'Stay close by my servants, until they have finished all my harvest.'"* [22] *Naomi said to Ruth, her daughter-in-law, "It is better, my daughter, that you go out with his young women, otherwise you might be bothered in another field."* [23] *So she stayed close to the young women of Boaz, gleaning until the end of the barley and wheat harvests; and she lived with her mother-in-law.*

Naomi is delighted to hear that Ruth's bounty has been due to the kindness of a man who is a near relative. Better, then, for Ruth to stay close to the young women who work for Boaz, so she will be safe. But she is not exempt from labor. She continues gleaning until the end of harvest.

Ruth lives at home, going out daily to earn her living. All the while she is becoming more integrated into the people she has chosen to join. She is forming friendships.

Her closeness to Boaz is deepening. The Lord of Israel is becoming more and more her personal God.

And here is where I must take up my own story in greater detail. In Carmel, I had received a basic kindness and acceptance. I had lived and worked with women who knew and loved God. I had gleaned quite a lot of personal "harvest" over the years. I had an adaptable and pleasant manner, a certain amount of natural talent. I "fit in" without too much fuss on the surface, but underneath I was very confused and disoriented.

Like Ruth who to the end remains "the Moabite," I had to come to terms with my own sense of "foreignness," of not quite belonging, of trying so hard to be absorbed into the group that I did not know how to be myself.

I needed to develop a sense of my own personhood, that essential self that had somehow been lost as I adapted to life. That loss was due, in part, to never having known my natural mother, and also through the well-meant deception that colored my upbringing and family history. My emerging personality seemed to me to have been formed by violence: the death of my mother and my own suffering at my difficult birth, the conflict with my family as I chose another church, the defiance I showed my father when I entered religious life as a teenager, the loneliness that came with transferring Orders and feeling myself the "outsider" even there...the list could go on endlessly.

Then, when I thought I could not go on as I was, that I would descend like Naomi into a sea of anger and despair, Providence sent someone who has been a true Boaz figure for me, a therapist who accepted me with kindness, encouraged me to discover my own truth and allowed me to drop the mask of the "competent Carmelite" and let my plain self beneath emerge.

I had been used to being told to forget the past, or to focus on my gifts rather than my weaknesses. Now I was encouraged to show my weakness and sinfulness without fear of judgment, to look at the motives for my

actions, the unhealthy ways I had of holding on to childhood images that skewed my perception of adult reality.

At that time, too, I had the opportunity to regularly
leave enclosure. I was able to distance myself from my
community, have space of my own, experience adult life
in the day-to-day world in which most people have to live
and work.

I had entered religious life young and unusually im-
mature because of my sheltered and bewildering childhood. I desperately needed others to validate me; I felt
safe in the group, with structure and rules and expecta-
tions that I understood. I needed security and God gave it
to me. Occasionally the violence within me, the sense of
alienation, would erupt, but my circumscribed lifestyle
kept this largely under control.

Traveling to London every two weeks for my therapy
sessions gave me a new sense of individuality. For the first
time, I met other adults as equals. I sat in the train watching my fellow passengers with interest; I walked through
London rather than take the subway just to be with ordinary people, to feel one of the large, diverse crowd, rather
than a person set apart in a special environment.

Living in enclosure reveals weakness and poverty in a
certain way. It can help us attune to the needs of others,
sensitizing the spirit to both the human and the divine.
But enclosure can also sometimes deaden the senses, turn
people in upon themselves and give an unreal security
through rules and laws that seem to remove free choice
and its attendant responsibility and risks. The effects of
enclosure depend on many variables, not the least of
which is the sort of person who undertakes this lifestyle.
For some, it is an ideal environment for spiritual peace; for
others, it merely magnifies the emptiness within.

The rhythm of going out and coming back; of being
with my community yet being apart has given me a new
understanding of myself. I have discovered a new respect
and love for others and for myself, just as Ruth must

gradually have become more aware, as the weeks of harvest passed, of her connection with those with whom she worked. Even if they were Israelite women, they were women the same as herself, with the same emotions, fears and needs.

Yet, Ruth would always remain the Moabite. She would have to integrate her own personal experience into this way of life she was now choosing, and would have to learn to choose it ever more freely and personally. She could never be other than she was, and much of her youth would be incommunicable to those who knew nothing of Moab.

This interval in the book of Ruth is a saga of blessing and grace, of Providence and provision, of work and rest, of coming in and going out, as Ruth negotiates her way into this new people. If it were not for this time of waiting, her love of Naomi and Boaz would prevent her growth. She would pass from dependency to dependency and not become her own woman, capable of relationships that enable her to surrender to others in love—person to person, whether to other humans or to God. With Naomi, Ruth has traveled far, but not far enough. Her destiny demands time for self-knowledge and self-acceptance before she can move on.

LORD,

in your loving providence
you give me time.
Teach me to use it well,
whether I am called to labor or to rest,
to sorrow or to joy.
There is a season for everything.
Help me to discern
when the time is right
for taking the next step,
and may I trust your guiding hand,
even when the waiting seems long
and my prayer unanswered.

PART THREE

Chapter Ten

A Plan Unveiled

> ¹ Naomi her mother-in-law said to her, "My daughter, I need to seek some security for you, so that it may be well with you. ² Now here is our kinsman Boaz, with whose young women you have been working. See, he is winnowing barley tonight at the threshing floor. ³ Now wash and anoint yourself, and put on your best clothes and go down to the threshing floor; but do not make yourself known to the man until he has finished eating and drinking. ⁴ When he lies down, observe the place where he lies; then go and uncover his feet and lie down; and he will tell you what to do." ⁵ She said to her, "All that you tell me I will do."

Naomi has tested the love of Ruth for her and the Israelite people. She has seen her develop and gain confidence. Her self-acceptance has reached the point where self-affirmation is in order. It is time for Ruth to be bold and take hold of her future with courage.

Naomi has lost all hope of bearing a child, but with Ruth married, descendants will be ensured for the family of Elimelech. Naomi needs Ruth to complete her now that she has lost her sons. Ruth has needed the love and example of good mothering to prepare her to become a mother herself. Each looks to the other to fill a void in their lives.

The Ruth-Naomi bond is unique in the Bible. It is caring, nonjudgmental, accepting, devoted, whereas mother-in-law and daughter-in-law might be expected to have some conflict and competition. Almost all other relationships among biblical women are fraught with jealousy and tension: Sarah and Hagar, Rachel and Leah, Hannah and Penninah.

The quest for a healing maternal relationship in order for Ruth to tap into her own maternal potential has been activated. For that love to be sustained and grow, it must move on to another stage. Ruth has left all to follow Naomi, now Naomi has to let Ruth go, indeed encourage her once more, as she did in Moab, to find her own home and her own life. Naomi's love has not engulfed Ruth in such a way that Ruth has been left without her freedom. Mind and heart combine to direct choices that will ultimately lead to fruitfulness for both women.

The end to barrenness, the blessing of fertility will belong to Ruth's new home, her new self. Becoming a mother is for her a yet uncharted journey, which Naomi has traveled already. Ruth has grown in readiness for marital responsibility and commitment. Naomi senses this and so outlines her plan for a husband. She is a gifted strategist.

First, Naomi invokes the levirate law by which a man should marry his brother's wife if she is childless. Boaz is not a brother-in-law, but he is a near relative. Naomi is too old for marriage. Ruth is a foreigner, yet Boaz has shown her kindness which may well be ripening into love. If he had not already behaved so generously Naomi might never have encouraged Ruth to approach him with such boldness.

It is threshing time, a time for feasting and merrymaking. To thresh the grain, that is, to separate the kernels from the stalks, the workers first scattered the sheaves over a dry, flat piece of ground (the threshing floor). They then beat the stalks with flails or drove a team of oxen over them, hitching the animals to a wooden sledge which had knobs of stone or metal underneath. The scraping of the sled loosened the kernels of grain and broke the stalks into chaff.

After this was done, the grain was winnowed by being lifted with a pronged fork or fanlike shovel. When tossed into the air, the wind blew away the lighter chaff while the grains of barley or wheat fell back to the ground. Winnowing was generally done in the evening when the breezes blew in from the Mediterranean and made the work easier. The winnowing completed, groups of women sifted the kernels through sieves to separate out the last pieces of chaff. The grain was then collected in earthenware jars for storage.

If a harvest had been good, there was every reason to celebrate. It meant a supply of food was ensured for the year, and because the labor lasted for several days, combined with singing and feasting, Naomi decided it was the best time to remind Boaz of his family obligations.

So Naomi instructs Ruth to wash and anoint herself. She is to dress in her best clothes and go down to the threshing floor. Presumably, she has until this point in time been wearing the garb of a widow. Colorful dress would mark her out as one proclaiming the end of her period of mourning. She could then be considered eligible for marriage once again.

At the threshing floor, says Naomi, Ruth must observe Boaz and see where he goes to rest. Then she is to "uncover his feet" and lie down. From here on Boaz will tell her what to do. He will initiate Ruth into whatever follows this night encounter. Ruth's part is to trust Naomi and the customs of her people.

In the biblical narratives about women a change of clothing is often a way to affirm a woman's dignity and self-worth. It shows she values her body and cares about how she presents herself to others. Queen Esther apparels herself in her finest robes before appearing before King Ahasuerus;[1] Judith does likewise before going out to meet Holofernes.

When Judith had stopped crying out to the God of Israel…she rose from where she lay prostrate. She called her maid and went down to the house where she lived on Sabbaths and on her festal days. She removed the sackcloth she had been wearing, took off her widow's garments, bathed her body with water, and anointed herself with precious ointment. She combed her hair, put on her tiara, and dressed herself in her festive attire.... Thus she made herself very beautiful.... When [the elders] saw her transformed in appearance...they were very greatly astounded at her beauty and said to her, "May the God of our ancestors grant you favor and fulfill your plans, so that the people of Israel may glory and Jerusalem be exalted." She bowed down to God.

Then she said to them, "Order the gate of the town to be opened for me, so that I may go out and accomplish the things you have just said to me." (Judith 10:1–4, 7–9)

Outer clothing reveals our sense of self. Judith is a woman who realizes the power she has as she faces the enemy looking beautiful and confident: the good wife in the Book of Proverbs is "clothed with strength and dignity,"[2] signified by her warm, handwoven apparel. Inner clothing pertains to the Spirit. Saint Paul exhorts the Colossians to be clothed in gentleness, kindness and compassion as a reflection of the Savior.[3] The baptized are to be clothed in Christ, in the "new self" made in God's image.[4]

These virtues are not always easy to hold together— real humility coupled with a proper self-respect reflected in demeanor and dress. Ruth's preparations to meet Boaz, her cleansing and anointing are, for the Christian, symbols of baptism. The garment she wears is a reminder of the white baptismal robe, which signifies purity and a new beginning. All Ruth does is in preparation for the encounter that will take place at the threshing floor this harvest time.

Ruth prepares herself to seize the opportunity offered to her. There are times for each of us that, if we let them pass, do not come again, at least, not in that precise way.

To be alert for these times, to listen to wise words yet make our own decision, demands discernment.

Saint Ignatius of Loyola spent a long time observing himself and others as he tried to formulate some rules which would help in the discernment process. If a decision is right, he found, there is a deep sense of peace about it, a sense of being encouraged to proceed. The Spirit of God brings calm patience, trust in God's power and strength to surmount difficulties. There is a sense of "homecoming," a sense that this is right for the individual and in tune with the will of God.

No life is static. And we must each ask ourselves, is this my time of decision? And if so, what is it to be? Ruth makes a choice that will determine her future as she steps out into the night and into the unknown.

LORD,

clothe me with yourself,
with compassion, kindness, humility,
gentleness and patience.
Make me alert to the opportunities life brings.
Don't let me refuse to go forward
through cowardice or the desire to play safe.
Make me willing to listen to the advice of
those who love me,
and above all to trust that you will guide me
along the way you have planned for me.
Let me grasp the opportunity
when the time is right
and go forward in trust.

Notes

[1] Esther 15:1–5.
[2] Proverbs 31:25.
[3] Colossians 3:12.
[4] Ephesians 4:24.

Chapter Eleven

MIDNIGHT ENCOUNTER

> *⁶ So she went down to the threshing floor and did just as her mother-in-law had instructed her. ⁷ When Boaz had eaten and drunk, and he was in a contented mood, he went to lie down at the end of the heap of grain. Then she came stealthily and uncovered his feet and lay down. ⁸ At midnight the man was startled, and turned over, and there, lying at his feet, was a woman! ⁹ He said, "Who are you?" And she answered, "I am Ruth, your servant; spread your cloak over your servant, for you are next-of-kin." ¹⁰ He said, "May you be blessed by the LORD, my daughter; this last instance of your loyalty is better than the first; you have not gone after young men, whether poor or rich. ¹¹ And now, my daughter, do not be afraid, I will do for you all that you ask, for all the assembly of my people know that you are a worthy woman. ¹² But now, though it is true that I am a near kinsman, there is another kinsman more closely related than I. ¹³ Remain this night, and in the morning, if he will act as next-of-kin for you, good; let him do it. If he is not willing to act as next-of-kin for you, then, as the LORD lives, I will act as next-of-kin for you. Lie down until the morning."*

Night has long been recognized as a sacred time. The bridegroom is to come at midnight in Christian tradition. The great festivals of Christmas and Easter are kept with a night vigil that emphasizes the sacredness and silence of the liturgical celebration. At night Jesus was

born in Bethlehem, where Ruth now comes to Boaz as he
sleeps on the threshing floor.

"My soul yearns for you in the night, / my spirit within
me earnestly seeks you" (Isaiah 26:9), are the words of the
prophet Isaiah. And Saint John of the Cross, speaks of
the soul going forth to seek the Beloved under cover of
darkness.

> Upon a darksome night,
> Kindling with love in flame of yearning keen,
> O moment of delight!
> I went by all unseen,
> New-hush'd to rest the house where I had been.[1]

So Ruth risks herself in this stealthy encounter with Boaz
that takes place in the darkness. She lies down beneath his
coverlet and waits for a response.

The sharing of a blanket or cloak is symbolic of be-
trothal. Here Boaz is being invited to spread his covering
over Ruth as a sign that she is to be his wife. He is invited
to shelter her just as she has sought shelter beneath the
wings of the Lord.

The prophet Ezekiel uses the same metaphor when he
speaks of Jerusalem, the beloved city. Jerusalem was orig-
inally a city of foreigners, but God had chosen it for his
own as he had chosen the people of Israel. It was because
of God's choice that Jerusalem became the city of the king
and the boast of the nations.

> Thus says the Lord GOD to Jerusalem: Your origin
> and your birth were in the land of the Canaanites;
> your father was an Amorite, and your mother a
> Hittite. As for your birth, on the day you were born
> your navel cord was not cut, nor were you washed
> with water to cleanse you, nor rubbed with salt, nor
> wrapped in cloths....
>
> I passed by you and saw you flailing about in
> your blood. As you lay in your blood I said to you,
> "Live! and grow up like a plant of the field." You
> grew up...and arrived at womanhood...I passed by

you again and looked on you; you were at the age for love. I spread the edge of my cloak over you, and covered your nakedness: I pledged myself to you and entered into a covenant with you, says the Lord GOD, and you became mine. (Ezekiel 16:3–4,6–7a,8)

Boaz now proceeds to choose the foreign woman beside him as God has chosen Jerusalem. And he chooses her with humble gratitude. Ruth could have reached out for the protection of a younger man who would promise more in the way of contemporary companionship and high spirits. She has instead chosen otherwise. Heart speaks to heart—Naomi's heart to the heart of Ruth, Ruth's heart to the heart of Boaz.

There is a sense in which God is grateful if we choose him. God does not force love upon us. God waits. God gives us our freedom. Ruth goes to Boaz to offer him all she has and is, just as the woman who anoints Jesus pours out on him the precious ointment that is the symbol of her love and devotion. It is superfluous, but it signifies a life given in love to the Redeemer.

When Mary is overshadowed by the Spirit at the Annunciation, God humbly asks for her consent to the great mystery that will be wrought in her flesh as she becomes the Mother of God. In asking Boaz to shelter her under his cloak, Ruth beseeches God, the ultimate Redeemer, to welcome her into the covenantal relationship God shares with the chosen people. By her words and example Ruth reveals that she has completed her initiation into Israelite custom and tradition. She is spiritually ready for assimilation. Like courageous Tamar she then risks herself in what might seem the seduction of a man by a woman.

Ruth is in a long line of women who, like Mary of Nazareth, are outside the ordinary run of things. Ruth does not encounter her future marriage partner in the security of home but under the purple harvest-moonlit heaven. She is not like Sarah in her tent, or Queen Esther in her palace; she is not the worthy wife in her well-kept home, guarding her sacred inner space. She seeks the answer to her own personal destiny out in the wild.

To "uncover the feet" in the ancient world was a euphemism for the sexual parts; what actually happened at the threshing floor between Ruth and Boaz is thus open to conjecture. But it would seem from what follows in the story that intercourse did not take place, although the situation was a compromising one and could be open to misinterpretation.

The book of Ruth conveys a sense of the genuine holiness and humility of its characters. Naomi yields to Ruth's pleading at the start of the narrative, Ruth yields to Naomi in her suggestion of marriage plans, Boaz yields to Ruth's audacity in claiming his protection. Each recognizes in events the hand of God and responds, so that the story unfolds within an ambience of mutual tenderness and selfless love.

When I was a child, I was, like many children, deeply sympathetic to those who were poor and suffering. I remember, in particular, a man with one leg who made his meager living selling pencils in a back street in Blackpool. I was heartbroken when my grandmother refused to buy a pencil from him, hurrying past and saying to me that you could be sure of better value in the shops. I went back home, locked the bathroom door behind me, and knelt on the floor, tears streaming down my cheeks, begging God to bless the man who had to stand on one leg like that, with no one showing compassion.

When I grew up I chose for myself a life on the margins as well as I knew how. But I discovered that I still was living within conventional limits as surely as if I were in a middle-class home.

So my journeys to London, my therapy, my growing self-knowledge and sense of identification with the really poor are challenging me to find ways to express my Carmelite vocation in a new form, a new call. I am more ready to risk myself and my security if that is demanded of me. I am still on the way and the outcome is unsure. I rely on God's fidelity and the faith I have that God will respond if I courageously reach out to approach the Divine Being who has chosen and called me first.

LORD,

prepare me to meet you in intimacy and love,
confident that you will not turn me away.
Help me to remember
that you desire to be loved and chosen
above all others.
If I show that I am serious in my intent
I know you will not fail me
or turn me away.
You have already spread your cloak over me,
but I have still to discover what this really entails:
the reality of a covenant love
which reciprocates your choice
and gives joy to your heart.

Notes

[1] John of the Cross, *Poems*, Complete Works, vol. II, E. Allison Peers, trans. (London: Burns Oates & Washbourne, Ltd., 1935), p. 417.

Chapter Twelve

NEWS FOR NAOMI

> ^{14} *So she lay at his feet until morning, but got up before one person could recognize another; for he said, "It must not be known that the woman came to the threshing floor."* ^{15} *Then he said, "Bring the cloak you are wearing and hold it out." So she held it, and he measured out six measures of barley, and put it on her back; then she went into the city.* ^{16} *She came to her mother-in-law, who said, "How did things go with you, my daughter?" Then she told her all that the man had done for her,* ^{17} *saying, "He gave me these six measures of barley, for he said, 'Do not go back to your mother-in-law empty-handed.'"* ^{18} *She replied, "Wait, my daughter, until you learn how the matter turns out, for the man will not rest, but will settle the matter today."*

The night encounter ends. Boaz has explained to Ruth that, happy as he is to wed her according to the Law, grateful as he is that she has chosen him, there is another male relative, who has so far not appeared in the story, who has a prior claim. As the man most closely related to Elimelech he must be given the opportunity to fulfill his obligations if he wishes.

The situation may not have been easy for Boaz to acknowledge, sometimes rules can get in the way of what we would naturally like to do. But Boaz is a man of honor and wants to have everything done as the Law prescribes. It is also a safeguard for the future. It will ensure that there are no recriminations or feuds over Ruth if the other man's rights are overlooked or ignored.

After Boaz has told Ruth of the legal requirements, she rests with confidence until the morning light is about to dawn over the fields. Then Boaz bids her rise and be on her way before she can be recognized and her actions mis-interpreted. She might be accosted by drunken harvest revelers or taken as a public prostitute.

As a sign of his goodwill, Boaz asks for Ruth's mantle, which women used as a head covering as well as a cloak. Up to this point, Ruth may well have been partially veiled. Now she takes the heavy veil away and the two can look at one another face to face. Night has enabled a very inti-mate conversation to take place, but light is now streaking over the distant horizon. It is almost dawn. Ruth and Boaz can gaze into one another's eyes for the first time. Boaz's eyes are full of gratitude, tenderness and concern, Ruth's eyes are alight with a shy joy and hope.

Into her outspread mantle Boaz pours six measures of grain, enough for both Ruth and Naomi. Then he folds the material into a sack for Ruth to carry on her shoulders. Should she be seen as she returns to the town, she will be taken for a woman who has risen early to perform the first task of the day—grinding corn for the family's bread. Then Boaz turns and makes his way back to Bethlehem alone, while Ruth, after his departure, turns in the direc-tion of Naomi's house.

When Naomi sees Ruth approaching along the dusty road that they had both trodden as they came back from Moab, she is all ears to hear what has happened at the threshing floor. Has Boaz responded as she hoped? Her question, "How did things go with you, my daughter?" means literally, "Who are you, my daughter?" That is, what is your condition? Are you now the promised wife of Boaz or are you still mine? Ruth responds with proof that she belongs to both as she opens her mantle. Boaz has claimed her and also given her enough grain for Naomi.

Her loyalties need not be divided. In gaining a husband Ruth does not lose the older woman who has become her best friend and mentor. The mother-daughter bond is intact while a marriage bond is about to be consummated.

As Naomi listens to Ruth's account of the night she knows that Boaz will not waste time but will settle the matter as soon as possible, indeed that very day. By claiming Boaz, even if she is technically incorrect, Ruth is set to enter the Israelite community through its ethical and religious structures, not just natural attraction.

Ruth and Naomi, vulnerable and insignificant widows, have revealed the heart of the Israelite community and of Israel's God. They have challenged men to live up to ideals that have been too often ignored. Their trust, their loving kindness toward one another are practical examples of how God wants the whole people to live in relation to the Divine.

Although inheritance is defined by the male line, it is often the women who ensure that the generations continue. Naomi has judged the situation aright. She has encouraged Ruth to risk herself. The risk is to be rewarded. Boaz will settle everything today.

How pregnant is the word *today*? Today is all that we have to serve God and to love others. How easy it is to put action off, to decide it is best to wait. If a decision is made and then we procrastinate, often that decision is never put into action at all. The opportunity passes; its importance recedes from consciousness. Why not just let things take their course? Why try to initiate change when things are all right as they are?

Saint Thérèse of Lisieux knew well the temptation to let things slide in an ordinary, humdrum life. She put it this way in one of her poems:

My life is but an instant, a fleeting hour above me,
My life is but a moment escaping swift away,
Thou knowest, O my God, on earth in time to love thee
I only have today.[1]

Boaz has surely become used to his bachelor life. It is flattering to have been approached by a young and beautiful woman in the darkness. But now, in the light of day, why should he consider changing his lifestyle to accommodate a wife? But the women in this story have taken steps to generate redemption, and now they trust it will happen, today.

So we leave Ruth and Naomi at home, waiting to see what will transpire. They have done what they could. They have trusted in Boaz's goodness and sense of honor. Now they must wait.

That is all we ourselves can do sometimes—trust in the Lord's goodness and justice and wait for our redemption. And if we are called upon in some way to redeem others by our actions, let us not waste time, but complete the business today, while time and life are ours.

LORD,

it's good to be able to share with friends
all that is happening in life.
Make my words words of encouragement
when others turn to me for a listening ear.
Let me have confidence
that you are guiding events
for the good of your people,
and that I have a part to play in the outcome.
If I am called upon to act for others,
don't let me put off the moment
when action is demanded of me.
And help me to appreciate the gift that is today.

Notes

[1] Thérèse of Lisieux, "My Song of Today," *Poems of Saint Therese*, vol. I, Carmelites of Santa Clara, trans. (London: Burns & Oates, 1925).

PART FOUR

Chapter Thirteen

BOAZ CONFRONTS THE NEXT-OF-KIN

¹ No sooner had Boaz gone up to the gate and sat down there than the next-of-kin, of whom Boaz had spoken, came passing by. So Boaz said, "Come over, friend; sit down here." And he went over and sat down. ² Then Boaz took ten men of the elders of the city, and said, "Sit down here"; so they sat down. ³ He then said to the next-of-kin, "Naomi, who has come back from the country of Moab, is selling the parcel of land that belonged to our kinsman Elimelech. ⁴ So I thought I would tell you of it, and say: Buy it in the presence of those sitting here, and in the presence of the elders of my people. If you will redeem it, redeem it; but if you will not, tell me, so that I may know; for there is no one prior to you to redeem it, and I come after you." So he said "I will redeem it." ⁵ Then Boaz said, "The day you acquire the field from the hand of Naomi, you are also acquiring Ruth the Moabite, the widow of the dead man, to maintain the dead man's name on his inheritance." ⁶ At this, the next-of-kin said, "I cannot redeem it for myself without damaging my own inheritance. Take my right of redemption yourself, for I cannot redeem it."

⁷ Now this was the custom in former times in Israel concerning redeeming and exchanging: to confirm a transaction, the one took off a sandal and gave it to the other; this was the manner of attesting in Israel.

⁸ So when the next-of-kin said to Boaz, "Acquire it for yourself," he took off his sandal.

Here we go with Boaz to the city gate while the women remain at home. This is clearly an ancient part of the narrative because the storyteller has to make a diversion and explain to his audience an old custom no longer in use.

Boaz goes to settle the matter before witnesses; he is determined to make public and honorable his private word. The city gate was the meeting point of any town's public life, almost anyone could be found there. At the gate caravans arrived and merchants haggled over merchandise; farmers and herdsmen gathered to buy and sell; current news and gossip were exchanged and disputes settled. "Elders," upright men deemed to be wise because of their many years, were designated as judges, and when there were accusations of crimes by one man against another or any kind of lawsuit to be settled the protagonists would meet at the city gate to argue the case and hear the verdict. The husband of the good wife in Proverbs is one "known in the city gates,"[1] just as Job mourns the loss of this prerogative in his time of suffering.[2] It was an honor to be chosen as "elder," and ten of these men together were a ready-made jury.

Boaz does not have long to wait before the man he seeks comes along. He calls him over and asks the elders to witness all he is about to say. He couches the confrontation in terms of a piece of land belonging to Naomi who has lately returned from Moab.

Boaz already appreciates the sterling qualities Ruth has shown. He is eager for marriage, but must conceal his real purpose to allay gossip, which could have been fostered by the favor he has shown Ruth during the harvest. So he approaches the topic by way of land rights, and only then does he speak of the levirate obligation.

Land is passed from one generation to another, but two lone women are unable to cultivate the field that belonged to Elimelech, so Naomi is selling it, says Boaz. The kinsman before him is more closely related to Naomi, will he "redeem" the land and keep it in the family or not?

The man readily agrees to do so. Extra land will mean extra wealth, extra prestige. Who would be so foolish as to pass up such an opportunity?

Then Boaz explains the "catch." The way the story is crafted allows readers to see the selfishness of the man who wants to redeem the land if it entails privilege, but not if it entails onerous obligations or a lessening of one's own rights. In this case, the one who redeems the field must also take the family's widow so as to raise up children who will bear the name of the deceased. That means that if the next-of-kin and Ruth have a son, the boy would take Elimelech's name and inherit the land when he reached his majority. In the meantime, the field might prove to be of no asset to the next-of-kin and his own heirs, and might even reduce his capital.

The kinsman draws back. Now that he knows the full conditions of sale, he is no longer interested. He would rather keep his own inheritance intact. Let Boaz take the land and the widow, for he is next in line.

To attest to the legality of the transaction the un-named kinsman removes his sandal and gives it to Boaz as a sign that he renounces his inheritance rights. Why a sandal? Maybe to signify that Boaz now can walk the land that he is buying in his kinsman's stead, and also that he has the right to sow the land that is Ruth's womb with his own seed.

The transaction is completed within the space of a few minutes. All is settled to the satisfaction of Boaz and those who are witnesses.

The unnamed kinsman remains without name throughout the whole story. He is, it seems, deemed un-worthy of remembrance because he is unwilling to be responsible. He considers only his own advantage.

So now Boaz has obtained what he set out to obtain—
Ruth. She is to be his bride, and together they will rebuild
the house of Naomi and Elimelech.

Although the book of Ruth does not mention this, the
genealogy in Matthew's Gospel preserves a tradition that
Boaz's mother was Rahab the harlot.[3] She was the one
who befriended the Hebrew spies when they came to re-
connoiter Jericho, and was responsible for the city being
taken, while her own family were saved by means of a
scarlet cord tied in the window. This Gentile background,
if true, might account for Boaz's inabililty to find a wife for
himself until now, and why Ruth would speak to his heart
as another woman who was suspect because of her racial
origins.

We are not used to seeing women as the "property" of
men as was common in the ancient world. Yet, we have
already been alerted to the fact that Boaz is no ordinary
husband who will dominate his wife, nor Ruth a meekly
compliant woman who does not know her own mind. In
the course of the story she has certainly become her own
person, capable of relating to others as an adult woman.
She is "bought" but only because she wants it to be so on
the legal level. Her heart is already given freely. Laws,
then, are meant to express a reality that is present rather
than bringing a new reality into being.

Laws can be a hindrance, and yet they are also a
safety. It can be difficult to have to go through the forms of
canon law to change one's position in an Order or transfer
to another Order, to obtain an annulment through a marriage tribunal, to ask advice on matters of conscience and
abide by church rulings. It is incumbent on those who are
responsible for these things not to prolong the suspense of
waiting indefinitely. But in the end there is wisdom in pro-
ceeding according to form.

I can feel hindered by laws and procedures when and
if I decide to take a new direction in my vocation; but this
is because I belong to a people and a community and they,

too, have rights and obligations that I must render to them
with a steadfast and humble heart.

LORD,

help me to give others their due
and not ride roughshod over their rights.
May I respect them
even if we see things differently.
And help me not to shirk responsibility
if others need to be protected or helped.
Give me the courage to be a redeemer,
even if it costs me in the process.

Notes

[1] Proverbs 31:23.
[2] Job 29:7.
[3] Matthew 1:5.

Chapter Fourteen

THE TRUE REDEEMER CLAIMS RUTH

⁹ Then Boaz said to the elders and all the people, "Today you are witnesses that I have acquired from the hand of Naomi all that belonged to Elimelech and all that belonged to Chilion and Mahlon. ¹⁰ I have also acquired Ruth the Moabite, the wife of Mahlon, to be my wife, to maintain the dead man's name on his inheritance, in order that the name of the dead may not be cut off from his kindred and from the gate of his native place; today you are witnesses." ¹¹ Then all the people who were at the gate, along with the elders, said, "We are witnesses. May the LORD make the woman who is coming into your house like Rachel and Leah who together built up the house of Israel. May you produce children in Ephrathah and bestow a name in Bethlehem; ¹² and, through the children that the LORD will give you through this young woman, may your house be like the house of Perez, whom Tamar bore to Judah."

The elders and all others at the city gate congratulate Boaz. He has taken the land. He has accepted the widow of Mahlon as wife (only at this point do we discover which of Naomi's two sons Ruth had been married to; she has not needed to be identified through a relationship with a particular man). Now Boaz will perpetuate the family line of Elimelech and all that has belonged to his

sons Chilion and Mahlon. The family that went away from
Bethlehem will have a perpetual remembrance in the very
town they had left.

A cry of blessing then goes up for Ruth. May she be as
one of the long line of Israel's womenfolk who have built
up the Hebrew people in their own day: Rachel, Leah and
Tamar. Ruth is wished the beauty and love that were
Rachel's, for she was the one for whom Jacob had labored
for seven years, yet "they seemed to him but a single day
because of the greatness of his love." [1] Leah is the fruitful
wife, the one who bore Jacob his first sons.[2] Tamar is the
woman who ensured Judah's inheritance and bore twins
by her father-in-law, so determined was she to have offspring. Of her twins, one put his hand out first during birth
and the midwife tied around his wrist a scarlet thread; but
then the hand was withdrawn and his brother emerged.
He was called Perez (a breach), claiming for himself the
inheritance of the firstborn.[3] Perez was an ancestor of
Boaz, another one who claimed his rights "out of turn."

Ruth is hailed among the people as a "young woman,"
not a widow. Now she is new-made for a new relationship.
As Boaz reflects the true Redeemer, so Ruth as a bride
mirrors the spouse that is Israel, all-glorious because chosen and beloved by God. Her virginity is restored. She is
whole again.

> Sing, O barren one who did not bear;
>   burst into song and shout,
>   you who have not been in labor!
> For the children of the desolate woman will be more
>   than the children of her that is married,
>   says the LORD....
> For you will spread out to the right and to the left,
>   and your descendants will possess the nations
>   and will settle the desolate towns.
>
> Do not fear, you will not be ashamed;
>   do not be discouraged, for you will not suffer
>   disgrace;

> for you will forget the shame of your youth,
>> and the disgrace of your widowhood you will
>>> remember no more.
> For your Maker is your husband,
>> the LORD of hosts is his name;
> the Holy One of Israel is your Redeemer,
>> the God of the whole earth he is called.
> (Isaiah 54: 1, 3–5)

Ruth is wished the fullness of fruitfulness and love. All blessings are, ultimately, for others, nurturing the human community, being generative in some way. Rachel, who had died at Bethlehem, is surrogate mother for the new life to be propagated in the same city by Ruth and Boaz.

No one is merely an individual. We each depend on others for life, growth, friendship, mutual love and care. I identify with the women of the Bible who struggle to be true to their vision, who claim their right to continue the line of promise in their own flesh. There are others, too, who are nameless—the women who surround and support Naomi and Ruth, the midwives who deliver the children, the widows who glean and gather, the barren who nurture a generation that is not their own progeny.

Then there are the women we meet in the gospels, Martha and Mary, the Samaritan women, Mary of Magdala, Mary of Nazareth, Joanna, Susanna, Jairus's daughter. Sometimes a fleeting glimpse, sometimes a longer narrative will bring these women to life. They are close to Jesus. He accepts them as they are, heals and inspires them. He is served by them and they, in their turn, listen to him and respond as faithful friends.

As a Carmelite I think, too, of the women who have preceded me in this way of life: the very first Carmelite women who made the same vows as the friars and lived them, each in their own way in their own homes; the first women who formed communities in Italy and the low countries in the fifteenth century. Not one name has been preserved, yet they were pioneers of a new way of living the Carmelite charism. What were their hopes and desires and dreams as they embarked on their own journeys of faith?

There are, of course, the truly "great" names of Carmel: Teresa of Avila, Thérèse of Lisieux, Elizabeth of the Trinity, Edith Stein. There are founders of active Carmelite sisterhoods who have added another dimension to the Order's presence among people in need. But there are many other women who just kept the Carmelite ideal going by playing their part in the daily round of prayer and work. These are women who come to mind most especially when I see a young woman making her vows, carrying on the life for those other sisters who are still to come in the future.

Then there are women who are particular to my own past, women who have inspired me and modeled for me what a woman can be. They have been married women, single women, teachers, community members. And they have encouraged me in my own growth and individuality, while reminding me that no one is self-sufficient. For each one I am grateful; for each one I thank God.

The blessing of Boaz and Ruth is a reminder of both our connectedness and our individuality. No person has exactly the same destiny. Each must live out their calling in their own way. And for the Christian, there is the reminder that we must abide constantly with Jesus, the one Redeemer, in whom alone we can bear the fruit that lasts for eternity.

LORD,

help me to be fruitful
in whatever way you want.
Let me be grateful for all I have received from others,
all who have been part of my own life,
and the life of my particular family and community.
And may I be a woman who blesses others
even as I have been blessed.

Notes

[1] Genesis 29:20.
[2] Genesis 29:32.
[3] Genesis 38:27–30.

Chapter Fifteen

JOY FOR NAOMI

¹³ So Boaz took Ruth and she became his wife. When they came together, the LORD made her conceive, and she bore a son. ¹⁴ Then the women said to Naomi, "Blessed be the LORD, who has not left you this day without next-of-kin; and may his name be renowned in Israel! ¹⁵ He shall be to you a restorer of life and a nourisher of your old age; for your daughter-in-law who loves you, who is more to you than seven sons, has borne him." ¹⁶ Then Naomi took the child and laid him in her bosom, and became his nurse. ¹⁷ The women of the neighborhood gave him a name, saying, "A son has been born to Naomi." They named him Obed; he became the father of Jesse, the father of David.

As the book of Ruth began with the theme of repentance and return, so it ends with the theme of redemption. Boaz has redeemed Ruth, and now Ruth redeems the bitterness of Naomi. Naomi is no longer Mara, the "bitter" one; she is "pleasant," a woman of joy. Ruth's love has given her a grandchild. Not only that, Ruth's love itself is honored. She is worth "more than seven sons," her loyalty and fidelity have been recognized by all.

Ruth has come into her own, and she brings Naomi into her orbit of fulfillment and blessing. In the Book of Samuel, Hannah rejoices that "the barren has born seven,"[1] whereas Ruth has borne only one. But she, as mother and daughter-in-law, is worth more than all the rest.

From the repeated use of the word "redeemer" in chapter 4, which culminates in the birth of Obed, Naomi's foster-son, we learn the importance of trusting in God, hoping against hope for redemption. When she returned to Judah, Naomi was blind to the seeds of hope that were there in the harvest fields of Bethlehem. But with Ruth's labor and devotion, Naomi has been enabled to respond to love offered. As her hope has been enkindled, so she has advised Ruth to approach Boaz. Thus, Ruth and Naomi together help themselves along the way of redemption. God uses them to redeem one another, and they see the process of redemption continue in the birth of Obed, father of Jesse.

God empowers us to struggle and to choose, to wrest blessings from life as life is given to us. God is there to aid us as we strive to move toward completion. But God will not do what we can do ourselves. God gives strength and light; God rekindles hope in the face of despair. As we take steps toward God, so God moves toward us.

The Bethlehem women who have witnessed the sour-faced return of Naomi from Moab, dispirited and despairing, now name Ruth's son as Naomi's own. It is the bond between Ruth and Naomi as much as the love of Boaz that is responsible for the infant's life. Obed is son to both. He is the tangible fruit of their friendship. Indeed, as there is no reference to Ruth's longing to conceive, it seems almost that God gave her a child in order to gladden Naomi. By claiming Obed as son, Naomi and Ruth enlarge their relationship, rather than being in competition over the longed-for heir. Ruth has fulfilled her destiny. The women of Bethlehem therefore name the child as one of their race and culture. Obed belongs to the land Ruth has made her own. Bonds between women have endured, and from these bonds the fabric of life has been woven.

Obed, whose name means "server," is Ruth's child through her waiting, her ability to endure and to labor. He is Naomi's son as heir of Elimelech. He is the bond between living and dead. Ruth has been the support of Naomi's grief, Naomi the instigator of Ruth's marriage to one she loves. Ruth has a home of her own, and Naomi rejoices. She is given the opportunity to cast aside her bitterness and return to her true identity. She has emerged from her mourning, thanks to the love of another who has proved faithful.

When did Ruth actually choose Naomi and her people rather than Moab? Sometimes she may have searched her memory for the moment when she knew beyond doubt that Naomi's life and her own would be forever bound together. It must have been long before the plaintive words, "Do not press me to leave you" were spoken at the borders of Moab and Judah.

In retrospect we can often see that decisions which come to light at a particular time have actually been made long before the choice is explicit. In my own life I look back and know that choices were forming before I was aware of them: choices of vocation, choices of good and bad ways of being and becoming. That is why I have needed help to bring these embryonic choices to the light of consciousness. I think I knew long ago that I wanted to discover a different way to live my Carmelite vocation. Only now am I finding the courage to claim and own that decision and find ways to make it a reality rather than a dream. Dreams cost nothing; dreams build nothing. Action is what counts, and we are formed by what we do and how we do it—as beings who can choose to "redeem" others, or to dam up the flow of life.

Sometimes I find myself to be a Ruth-figure: a follower, a lover, a woman striving to claim her individuality. At other times I am Naomi: bitter, deprived, mourning, yet allowing myself to know joy through others, bringing others along to new places. At other times I am Boaz: tenderly reaching out to those who are in need, confident in my worth, honorable and gentle. I discover the masculine elements in my personality through men I love, and am thereby strengthened.

I hope to incarnate the loving kindness of God in my own life, to be attentive to Providence in the day-to-day meetings and tasks that form me for eternity. God has always been for me an absent God and that is why the book of Ruth speaks to my heart. God is there but un-named. God remains in the shadows. I rest under the Divine wings but cannot see a face. It is in the love of those whom I love and who love me that God comes. God is the Redeemer who asks everything: loss of home, of land, of security, status and rights, so that I might cleave to God in the darkness of the night, and find God in the day of work and prayer. I have not arrived, but I keep going: forever an "outsider," yet one of the people of God by choice and vocation. For the outcome I still wait, but the choice is made.

And what of Orpah who was there with Ruth at the beginning and who made another choice? Surely she, too, in Moab, is rejoicing in her own life, although it has taken a different shape. Wherever she is, and however she decides to live, she is forever bonded to the two women whose love saw them through tragedy and loss to the other side, and to the claiming of redemption.

O sweetest love of God, too little known,
whoever finds you finds rest.
Let everything change, O my God,
that I may rest in you.
Everywhere with you, O my God,
everywhere all things with you as I wish.
All sweetness and delight for you, none for me;
all bitterness and trouble for me, none for you.

O my God, how sweet to me your presence
who are the sovereign Good.
I will draw near to you in silence and uncover your feet,
that you may unite me to yourself
making my soul your bride.
I will rejoice in nothing until I am in your arms.
O my God, I beseech you, leave me not for a moment,
because I know not the value of my soul.
— John of the Cross[2]

Notes

[1] 1 Samuel 2:5.

[2] Adapted from John of the Cross, *The Prayer of the Enamored Soul*, David Lewis, trans. (London: Thomas Baker, 1906).

Afterword

18 Now these are the descendants of Perez: Perez became the father of Hezron,19 Hezron of Ram, Ram of Amminadab,20 Amminadab of Nahshon, Nahshon of Salmon, 21 Salmon of Boaz, Boaz of Obed, 22 Obed of Jesse, and Jesse of David.

The book of Ruth ends with an addition that does not belong to the original text. It is an afterword to explain why Ruth is an important figure in Israel's history—she is the great-grandmother of King David. The genealogy traces the descent of the king. Ruth was the progenitor of Israel's royal house, though at the time she could never have guessed it. Her blood flows in the veins of David and those who succeed him.

But surely there is more to the story than this! Ruth is a woman to be revered in her own right. Even if she had nothing to do with David, is her history not worth remembering and celebrating? Yes, but here we can see how God used her in the Divine plan. Her human actions were directed toward a Divine destiny, and unknowingly, she cooperated. Her story bridges the era of Israel as family or tribe and Israel as a nation. Through Ruth the saga of the chosen people not only continues but stands on the brink of a new beginning.

There has been all along a sense of Divine direction worked out through human interaction, for from Ruth's descendants will come the Messiah. He is born in the same town as David, and he brings Jew and Gentile together in one body. The small city set on a hill south of Jerusalem has an eternal significance, and so it will remain through all generations. In those generations we, too, have a part.

We are preparing for those who will come after us and will ask us where the King of the Jews is born.

Many years after Ruth, shepherds would be watching their flocks in the same fields in which she had gleaned as a foreigner, and at the same time of night she had approached the sleeping Boaz.

Bethlehem is forever. The story of Ruth is for now and always. For each one of us is to be a herald of the coming of Christ, and by our daily lives we make the way ready for him through acts of loving kindness and truth.

> But you, O Bethlehem of Ephrathah,
>   who are one of the little clans of Judah,
> from you shall come forth for me
>   one who is to rule in Israel,
> whose origin is from of old,
>   from ancient days.
> Therefore he shall give them up until the time
>   when she who is in labor has brought forth;
> then the rest of his kindred shall return
>   to the people of Israel.
> And he shall stand and feed his flock in the
>   strength of the LORD,
>   in the majesty of the name of the LORD his God.
> And they shall live secure, for now he shall be great
>   to the ends of the earth;
> and he shall be the one of peace. (Micah 5:2–5a)

Bibliography

Anderson, Bernhard. *The Living World of the Old Testament*. London: Longman Group, 1988.

Craghan, John. *Esther, Judith, Tobit, Jonah, Ruth*. Wilmington, Del.: Michael Glazier, 1982.

John of the Cross. *Complete Works*, vol. II. E. Allison Peers, trans. London: Burns Oates & Washbourne, 1935.

—. *Complete Works* vol. II. David Lewis, trans. London: Thomas Baker, 1906.

Julian of Norwich. *Revelations of Divine Love*. J. Pichler, trans., unpublished manuscript.

Kates, Judith A. and Gail Twersky Reimer. *Reading Ruth: Contemporary Women Reclaim a Sacred Story*. New York: Ballantine Books, 1994.

Linafelt, Tod. *Ruth*. Collegeville, Minn.: Liturgical Press, 1999.

McCarthy, Carmel and William Riley. *The Old Testament Short Story: Explorations Into Narrative Spirituality*. Collegeville, Minn.: Michael Glazier, 1986.

Peck, M. Scott. *The Road Less Traveled*. London: Arrow Books, 1990.

Teresa of Avila. *Collected Works*. E. Allison Peers, ed. and trans. London: Sheed and Ward, 1972.

Thérèse of Lisieux. *Selected Poems*. Carmelites of Santa Clara, trans. London: Burns and Oates, 1925.

Wijngaards, J. N. M. *Inheriting the Master's Cloak: Creative Biblical Spirituality*. Notre Dame, Ind.: Ave Maria Press, 1985.